In Place of Fear II

A Socialist Programme
for an Independent Scotland

Jim Sillars

Vagabond Voices
Glasgow

First published in January 2014 by
Vagabond Voices Publishing Ltd.,
Glasgow,
Scotland.

ISBN 978-1-908251-30-5

Cover design by Mark Mechan

Typeset by Park Productions

For further information on Vagabond Voices, see the website,
www.vagabondvoices.co.uk

To: Jim & Celia

Jim Sillars

For my grandchildren – Stephen, Roseanne, Matthew, Lena, Rebecca, Josephine, Beth, Peter, John and Adam – whose love, affection and companionship have been the greatest gift of my life, and for Litster Gardiner who was a founder member of the SLP. Everyone in that party knows the immense debt of gratitude we owe him for the work he did. That the SLP died was no fault of his. That its members, who were enriched by the SLP experience, have continued to contribute to society in various walks of life, including politics, is something I hope he can be proud of.

And in memory of the late Bill McCrorie – a remarkable man, full of wisdom, who sought no publicity, but was a tireless worker for the SLP, a tower of strength and a source of encouragement as we fought together to keep socialism alive in South Ayrshire – and Stephen Maxwell, mourned by those who knew that an intellectual light had gone out when he died, and regretfully never permitted to be a candidate for the Scottish Parliament, denying that body the benefit of one of the finest minds this nation has produced.

And in special memory of Steve Butler who died just before Christmas. Missed by me, and many – the wisest of us all.

The content herein is my responsibility, but this is far from being a solo job. I have over many, many months had the opportunity to canvass opinions, entered into discussion, received ideas and criticisms from a large number of people offering a wide range of opinions, and I am grateful to them all. As many cannot be identified, I thought it best, with the exceptions above, to name no names.

For those, mostly in the media, who have no interest in the ideology of socialism, the Appendix sets out the main policy proposals, from which they can track back into the body of the text to find the justification for each one.

In Place of Fear II

A Socialist Programme
for an Independent Scotland

Contents

Foreword   1

In Place of Fear II   5

Acknowledgements   95

Foreword

The referendum is about power. On 18 September, 2014, between the hours of 7 am and 10 pm, absolute sovereign power will lie in the hands of the Scottish people. They have to decide whether to keep it, or give it away to where their minority status makes them permanently powerless and vulnerable.

Without sovereignty, Scotland is inherently weakened. Oil, gas, energy, whisky, land and other vital national interests are externally owned, often by those who do not put Scotland's interests first. Without the power to intervene in the national interest, a power available through independence, not devolution, we are at the mercy of forces that have no concern for us, our welfare or our future.

Independence alone can remedy this.

This subordinate position cannot be allowed to continue. Bereft of sovereign power we are in a trap, with others deciding the fate of our economy and society. The only way we can have a vision of a better tomorrow for our children and grandchildren, and deliver it to them, is by being a nation in full charge of itself.

Independence does not mean more of the same, with the only difference being that the saltire flies alone on public buildings instead of alongside the union flag. Independence is a paradigm shift. It means no longer tolerating the intolerable. It means using the power of the nation to create a different economic model than the present one that has failed us, and from there going on to build a decent society.

Remember the lesson of Grangemouth. On 24 October 2013, James Cook, reporting for BBC 1 pm news, summed up the position: 'The nation awaits the decision of one man.' A vital national interest to be saved or destroyed by a foreign billionaire. What a humiliation: one man vs 5 million, and the 5 million were powerless. There can be no better example of why that sovereign power in Scottish hands on 18 September must be retained, and why the socialist ethic of public good above all must again be embraced.

Grangemouth is not alone in showing that a new political and economic model is needed, where the public interest registers, where policies driven by the greed that has become so prevalent in the UK are replaced by ones founded on co-operation and concern for communities, and where a dynamic state is a powerful driver to achieve more equality.

The alternative to independence is more of the same. A land of food banks, pay-day loan companies and unremitting poverty for 250,000 children. Better Together is a fraudulent slogan. If Scots vote NO, they will be voting to be Poorer Together. The United Kingdom is heading towards a national debt of £1.5 trillion. The present 'recovery' is artificially stimulated and fuelled by more national and personal debt. It is designed to hide the truth and take the Tory Party successfully through the election campaign in 2015 – immediately thereafter the real cuts will come in. At present only £1 in every £10 of cuts has fallen upon the people. After the 2015 election, with £25 billion cuts scheduled in 2015-16, will come the deluge. The gap between the rich and the rest will grow wider.

Socialist ideas can change all that, with independence. Socialists have a vision, not an airy-fairy one where words compensate for lack of ideas, but one grounded on a programme that aims to shift power to working people and their families; that aims to end the indignity and corrosive effect of unemployment on the personality. A programme that will set people free from fear, that transforms the lives of those in poverty by abolishing it, that gives our young people a society in which they can develop all of their talents, that addresses the disabled with compassion, and that ensures dignity and security in old age for our pensioners.

What Scots have lacked to date is belief in their own power. Working people have allowed themselves to be browbeaten and manipulated into believing that this is the best of all possible worlds and that they are powerless to alter it. The myth of Scottish inadequacy has sapped the moral and political strength of the nation, and made it susceptible to swallowing lies about itself.

That depressing era comes to an end when, on achieving independence, Scots own their own country, are beholden to no one, bend the knee to no one, ask permission of no one for policies the people need, when they can think new thoughts, embrace new ideas and use the power that lies latent within themselves to change things for the better forever.

In place of fear we will create a nation proud, self-confident, prosperous, in which the working people will have the opportunity to exert their power to quickly build a fair and just society.

This is a programme of priorities. It concentrates on what must be done and can be done in short order.

In Place of Fear II

Sensible Socialism and Audacity

In 1952 Nye Bevan published *In Place of Fear*. He addressed a country in which fear of unemployment haunted the working class, whose experience of the 1930s had left bitter memories. Today, with the technological revolution gathering pace, job security seemingly a thing of the past, and labour just another commodity for sale or disposal in the marketplace, fear is back. It need not be so.

Nye Bevan did not argue against a mixed economy, but sought to conquer the commanding heights in order that the public good, through public control, brought benefits of production and services to the people. There are still considerable, if not actually commanding, heights to be conquered for the public good.

Time and circumstances have changed. China and the rest of Asia were still basket cases when *In Place of Fear* was published. Global capitalism through the transnational companies had yet to develop. So socialists today are faced with a very different world to that of the 1950s. We do not need to fear it.

Nye Bevan said that to succeed socialists must be audacious. We must be able to think and do what the establishment says we must not think and cannot do. There is, in fact, nothing the people cannot do when they exercise their power in an independent parliament. It is that power, with the audacity to use it, that this programme calls into action.

Paying for the Socialist Programme

This programme is coherent. The bits fit together. A number of projects will cost no more than money at present in the system. It will be better distributed and used. Resource management will, with a different economic model, maximise the assets of the nation, achieve higher growth rates, and increase the revenues for government. There are new ideas on funding.

It must be emphasised that tackling inequality and poverty requires not only growth but redistribution of wealth from the rich, including the corporate rich, to poorer sections of the community. No socialist government could run away from that reality.

Here are some examples of where finance will be better used. The Crown Estate will be nationalised. It will be called Scotland's Estate. And its wealth and income, and its potential additional income, will be paid directly to the Scottish Government. The management of Scotland's Estate, including the five rural estates with 37,000 hectares of land, 5,000 of forestry and mineral, salmon fishing rights, half the foreshore and all the sea bed, will be examined to see where it can better fit into the new policy of enhancing the public interest. It will be directly responsible to the Scottish Cabinet.

Scottish Enterprise will close. Its staff, their skills and abilities will not be lost in redundancy. Some staff will be transferred to the trade division in a Scottish Foreign Service, which will be funded by the repatriated Scottish contribution to the UK FCO, thus producing a nil additional cost. Other staff will form a Research Centre serving the Scottish Cabinet Office, assisting in the formulation of policy.

Scottish Development International will continue to be the lead organisation seeking inward investment, and will operate out of Scottish embassies. The savings from Scottish Enterprise closure will be around £200 million per year, and become part of the SME Ministry budget.

There will be state activity in creating jobs, and improving the financial position of the unemployed. When the capitalist system hits crisis, as it does, and fails, as it does, it does not mean that the needs of society disappear along with the fall and elimination of the incompetent and corrupt corporate giants. In the face of crisis for the people thrown out of work, the action to create jobs by state activity is based on the logic that it is a foolish waste to pay someone not to work, when well organized work can be provided that meets needs in the community, adds value to the community, and brings dignity and self-respect to the individual. How much better to pay someone the living wage to work than pay subsistence level to keep him or her in or near poverty.

Those people with more money in their pockets because they have a proper job will spend more in the community, and that spending, along with that of others, will create more jobs, which in turn will create further jobs and increase government revenue from VAT. The reverse happens when people are placed on the dole and given the lowest possible level of financial support, while we watch local shops close and depression set in.

Where additional money is required, an innovative system of bond issues will be employed, beyond the standard government gilts, where, as with house building for rent and the purchase of an oil company, there will be solid collateral for low risk specialised bonds at reasonable yield levels.

In the education field, on top of the money reallocated, the idea emanating from the work of Professor Lindsay Paterson 'Outstanding Students and Philanthropic Contributions in Scottish School Education', will be pursued by the government. Philanthropists will be urged to engage, not only with the exceptional students covered by Professor Paterson's work, but with some of the outstanding problems in some areas in which schools are located. Many already do so. Those who object to such philanthropy in the public sector will, no doubt, make sure they avoid those libraries and public halls which bear the name Carnegie, and no doubt Cumnock Academy should have rejected the cash from the New Cumnock lad Tom Hunter, when he sought to aid education in that part of Ayrshire.

Demolishing the Myth

It is constantly asserted, as though it was a knock-out blow to independence, that an independent Scotland would not have been able to withstand the crash of RBS and the Bank of Scotland. But when that happened there was no independent Scotland, so it is a false argument that has been allowed to gather strength due to the SNP government failing to point out its obvious flaw.

How can an independent Scotland that didn't exist be found incapable, when it didn't exist? Perhaps a question for philosophers, certainly not for grown-up, serious people.

RBS and Bank of Scotland failure was Westminster's failure. Westminster did not rescue them out of concern for Scotland's reputation in the financial world. Only around 10% of RBS was connected to Scotland, whereas 80% of the liabilities lay outside. Westminster Governments failed utterly to properly regulate the banking sector, allowing the banks to gamble with criminal recklessness – Scotland won't.

There will be no bank crashes in an independent Scotland. The banks will be divided between retail and investment. Each one will be required to have a 'public interest' director on the board, and they will be closely monitored. There will be a bi-annual stress test of each bank carried out by the SMA, with the statutory right to see the books fully opened. This stress test will apply to board and senior managers, who will be rigorously examined as to competence.

The Currency and Bank Governance Issues

Fiddling with Fiat Money

Scots for independence have been lectured by the Bank of England and the Treasury about how foolish it would be to get out from under their control. Given their record of incompetence, such an assertion is breathtaking. They were forecasting growth when the financial tsunami was half way across the Atlantic. Others saw it coming (including this author); they did not. They have sanctioned and engaged in printing money. They have invented money. If they were businesses and not government institutions, some of their practices would lead to jail.

Take QE: interest-bearing government bonds issued by the Treasury, and bought by banks and other institutions. These bonds are then bought by the Bank of England from these groups. The Treasury, a government department, then pays the Bank of England, a government institution, the interest on the bonds which totalled £35 billion. Then, as has happened, the Treasury calls on the Bank of England to pay it the £35 billion, which it then claimed as new income. Voila! A big chunk out of the fiscal deficit.

Fiat money is a piece of paper with no intrinsic value. Take a £5 note to a bank and ask it to honour the pledge that in exchange for your note it will pay five pounds sterling. You will get back another £5 note promising the same thing. The lesson is that governments can do anything they like with fiat money, as long as they can cast a spell upon the community to keep believing the paper has value. The Treasury and the Bank of England must have breathed a sigh of relief when no one questioned how that £35 billion came to exist. As for what happens when they start to unroll QE, they haven't a clue.

Currency

The idea that an independent Scotland should put itself under the permanent control of the Bank of England is so ludicrous, it is amazing it has been given any consideration.

The Monetary Policy Committee of the Bank of England has nine members. Five are drawn from within the Bank, and four additional ones appointed by the Chancellor of the Exchequer. Six of the nine went to Oxbridge. Only one has any past connection outside the bubble of the South of England. The Governor and one other come from the Goldman Sachs stable, and one is from the CBI. All anchored in London.

Does anyone seriously think that planking a lone Scot in among that lot will, in any way, alter their priority, which is London and its City?

Scotland needs a separate currency on independence. It will be necessary to align it with sterling in a transition phase, probably 5-8 years, to enable cross-border trade to carry no additional exchange costs, and to produce stability in the early stages of independence.

The argument between the Scottish Government and Westminster over currency has obscured a fact: if Scottish business wants to use the pound sterling instead of the Scottish currency for trading purposes, it is perfectly free to do so without being in a currency union. Sterling is a convertible currency like the euro and the US dollar. All over the world, for example, the US dollar is used for payments in trade. Transaction between Scots and English business in sterling will be no different – indeed normal.

The First Minister says that on independence there has to be a share-out of assets and liabilities. That is true. The national debt is a liability, and has to be shared. But he is mistaken when claiming sterling as an asset capable of being shared. Currency is a badge of sovereignty, issued by a sovereign nation, which decides whether it is convertible or not. A currency union means shared sovereignty, with a single central bank in control of each currency member. A currency union means Scotland gains sovereignty, then gives it away again. It also requires Westminster to share its sovereignty, most unlikely.

The difference between having a Scottish currency and our position in sterling now, is that a separate currency will, as we come to the end of the transition phase, achieve what a Yes vote is about – economic sovereignty.

No Independent Central Bank

Those who revel in the Central Banker title, and act as though they live among the Gods as the Lords of Finance, have been the problem not the solution to the world's economic condition. It was the hubris of Alan Greenspan, at the head of the US Federal Reserve, that was responsible above all others for the financial crash in 2007-08.

Like Singapore, there will be a Scottish Monetary Authority (SMA) which will supervise and regulate the banks, and oversee and approve the issue of Scottish currency notes by the banks in Scotland, with each issue backed by international reserves of dollars, yen, sterling, euro.

The statute of the SMA will give it wide latitude in its operations, as is necessary, as it will work within a global financial world, but *the SMA will not be an independent entity*. It will be responsible to the Scottish Finance Minister, who will appoint its senior management. The head of the SMA, in any dispute between the SMA and the Finance Minister, over any direction which the latter wishes to issue, will have the right of audience before the full Scottish cabinet.

Scottish Socialism will be renewed by the challenge of independence

'All our Socialist dreams have been destroyed by the London connection.'
Retired miner, Netherthird, Cumnock, 1979

Changing for the Better Forever

That old miner had, and has, a point. The socialist movement in Scotland has never been able to pursue its policies here because no matter how we vote in the elections in which lie real power, those for Westminster government, the Scottish tail can never wag the southern dog. Even when Labour had 50 MPs out of 79, it was powerless to prevent attack after attack on the Scottish people because England voted Tory.

How many times are the Scots willing to go to the polls, vote for the government they want, and end up with the government they rejected? Happens in the UK. Cannot happen in an independent Scotland.

Even when, in the Blair–Brown years, there was a New

Labour Government at Westminster, its policies were dictated by concern for the views of Middle England, with Scotland important only for the number of our MPs that would troop through the division lobbies. Scotland for British Labour has been the land of the lobby fodder.

The prospect of independence opens possibilities previously closed. This programme sets out a socialist vision of an independent Scotland. Not utopian, but a realistic one aimed at giving power to the working people and their families, so that they can create a decent society based on values of egalitarianism, wherein no one starves or goes in fear of unemployment, and our young people can be ambitious, and successful in their own country.

We live in a world where the capitalist ethic seems to be triumphant. How this can be, given the crisis that broke in 2007, the manifest inability of those who believe in the efficacy of market forces to solve that crisis, and the socialisation of the banking system, is a mystery. Perhaps not a mystery, as the socialist movement has been dormant intellectually for some time, and allowed the pernicious nostrums of the ideological children of Mrs. Thatcher to go unchallenged.

It is time to challenge capitalism once again, and this programme does so. It sets out why socialist ideas are relevant to Scottish economic life, and how they will release thousands of families from the grip of fear.

The Core Issues

This programme addresses the core issues that determine the life styles, life expectancy, welfare, prosperity and opportunities for our young people in a Scotland that, on independence, will put Scots in control of their own destiny for the first time in over 300 years. The issues are: people, education, jobs, the welfare state, and land use.

Independent Scotland should not bow to the God of capitalism, but nor can we ignore it. This programme looks at socialism in the twenty-first century and seeks to address honestly the circumstances we face, and the sometimes bitter lessons history has taught us. We cannot afford the luxury of past patterns of politics, with its indulgence of rhetoric that has no intellectual foundation.

Before the Attlee Government, and after it, social-ist leaders in the shape of Labour Governments were bold on rhetoric before coming to office, but quickly caved in to pressures in the capitalist system because they were intellectually unprepared. There are those today who would place themselves well to the Left, who revel in their self-proclaimed radicalism, and love to rant against neo-liberalism, who are as intellectually sterile as those Labour failures.

Rhetoric is not policy, and nor is policy when it avoids the realities which any socialist government will have to cope with. With a proper solid foundation of ideology anchored in reality, we socialists can change this nation for the better, forever.

Sensible Socialism

Given the dearth of discussion and examination of ide-ology in the last thirty years or so, it is necessary, before spelling out concrete ideas, to spend some time in addressing how we rethink socialism in the twenty-first century, which is profoundly different from the twentieth century when democratic socialism developed and flourished – until its near death experience under New Labour, with its worship of the market.

Socialism today can be defined as action to advance labour's ability to prevent its exploitation by capital, secure a distribution of wealth and power that favours working people and promotes co-operation which can be achieved through social ownership and by exerting public control over parts of the economy vital to the interests of the people.

If socialism is to guide policies in Scotland in this century, it must be based on realism – a guide not a dogma. This is no time for empty slogans. We need sensible socialism. It is time to think. Socialists must acknowledge that wealth creation determines the value and scale available for redistribution because, in recent years what passes for the Left, as it faced deindustrialisation, has concentrated its energies in defending the public sector. Between 1997 and 2007, investment in the public sector rose by 53%, yet when the crunch came, and the fragility of the economy that underpinned it was exposed, public sector workers' pensions and wages came under direct attack. The link between the wealth-generating economy and sustainable public services must always be factored into policy.

There is one important point socialists must get across to people. It is a dangerous, powerful myth that the private sector creates wealth, whereas the public sector spends it. Carefully directed spending by the state multiplies and creates wealth too.

Are we really to believe that a medical team which

puts a young person back into work after a serious accident, does not contribute more to wealth creation than does a currency speculator? Is the engineer who services a railway track not as much involved in the creation of wealth as the worker who runs the train along it? There is an intimate interplay between public services and the private sector, and one cannot function without the other.

Time to end Timidity
Time to be Bold

Socialism in one country is not possible in a world where many economies are intertwined, and global trade policy, including intellectual property and services, is governed by the rule-based World Trade Organisation. So what do socialists do in a small country like Scotland? Throw in the towel, cave in to the doctrine of market forces, as New Labour did, pin their hopes on low corporation tax so they can hawk their country round the world for foreign investment bringing any kind of jobs at any low level of wages, and abandon any hope of policies that promote the interests of those who sell their labour, whether it be by physical or mental effort? No.

The basic truth that governs most lives, lost sight of in recent years, is the ability or inability of people to sell their labour. Yes, the state can ensure a minimum of living standards for those out of work, but that does not free people from poverty and anxiety. They are not in control of their lives; they are truly subjects of the state.

Socialism has been in retreat. Scorn is poured upon those who dare challenge the notion that markets are the most rational system for the allocation of resources, and upon those who assert that the idea of collective solidarity has value. It is no accident that as socialism has retreated from the public arena, greed, the inevitable consequence of the idea that the individual should look only to self-interest, has been the most marked feature of our unequal society.

Socialists have grown timid in the face of trans-national capitalism, and the neo-liberal boasts asserting the superiority of market forces. As we watch the great flows of capital around the world, the rise of the global companies, the power that they seem to exert as the prime movers and shakers above and beyond the control of politicians and states, it is understandable that the answer to the question 'What is to be done?' is 'Not much we can do.' Wrong.

Capitalism and Socialism

Socialists should respond to the role of capital by recognising that we are dealing with two quite different phenomena, both in scale and character. Big capital comes in the shape of large companies, many with a global reach, and there is capital anchored in the community in the SME sector. They call for different policies.

International capital and its global company giants are not as powerful as they seem, provided we understand that as well as strengths they have weaknesses, and that as well as weaknesses states have power. The idea that when challenged via taxation or regulatory policies or laws to protect workers, all global companies will up stakes and depart for elsewhere, is infantile. But before looking more closely than is usually the case at the relative strengths of capitalism and the nation state, we should look objectively at why capitalism has been successful when compared to the failure of a centrally managed Soviet-style system, or the hybrid of state capitalism and Quango management – the traditional Labour government method.

Despite the theories of the outside Left, capitalism is not a system run by evil men and women, who sit down together plotting to do harm to the multitudes. It is a system which has the search for profit as its driving force. It is to date the most successful economic system produced by humankind.

It has generated and released great technical and productive forces on a scale never seen before, and it has in many countries transformed the living and health standards of billions of people. It has, of course, a characteristic that is not often admitted by its adherents (except by the Austrian school), in that it requires renewal through constructive destruction – that is, those who fail in the market should be allowed to fail, leaving room for others to emerge and flourish, rather like the fall of diseased great trees enables new growth in the forest. Where it has flourished, so has the rule of law.

But capitalism is not an unalloyed benefit to human beings. Hugh MacDiarmid described it as a 'leper pearl' that tarnishes everything to which it does not bring its blessings. Big Capital in pursuit of profit exploits labour, plays off people against people, governments against governments, and, where a state is weak, is rapacious in its use of children and misuse of resources and the environment. It is a system that frequently gets out of balance, creating economic and social crisis on a large scale, with much human misery as the consequence. There are, of course, enlightened capitalist organisations that recognise the importance to them of labour, but as many an employee of an enlightened outfit has found when a crunch arrives, their interests are the first to be jettisoned.

Capitalism and its concomitant of market forces free to roam are managed by people who no doubt have a moral compass guiding their private lives, but operate a system governed by an amoral principle: investment will take place only when it can produce a profit. This is not an attack on profit per se, merely stating a fact. That fact has consequences. As the economic crisis grew, and there was a clamant need for investment to kick-start the recovery, corporate Britain sat on £750 billion in cash because it saw no real prospect of growth and profits. The national interest didn't come into their calculations or motivation.

When workers withdraw their labour, there is a great stramash with warnings of the economic cost to the national GDP. A 'strike' of capital is hardly remarked upon.

Where, however, there is prospect of profit, investment will follow, as it has done with the pay-day loan companies which are expanding their reach as they feast upon the needs of the poor. There may be on many occasions a social benefit arising out of an investment, and it will be painted as such by the PR departments, but that is window dressing. When profit is threatened, or profit can be maximised by a shift of location, social benefits receive lip service but don't count – ask the Diageo workers at Kilmarnock.

If we see profit as surplus value after the costs involved in economic activity have been met, there can be no objection to it. Companies without profit go bust. State enterprises without profit make a claim on state revenues and capital, leading to malinvestment – as has happened in China on a grand scale. It is what is done with the 'profit' that matters. If a good part of it is ploughed back into an economic activity, particularly in research and development, whether it be a private company or a state-owned one, there is national benefit.

Unlike capitalism, socialism does have a moral purpose. In its basic theory socialism seeks to replace the weakness and latent insecurity of labour by controlling capital in the interests of the general community, the vast majority of which are workers without wealth. Its purpose is to create a society that is fair, where there is no reason for poverty, and where the standard of living and the cultural level of the people are uplifted. Critics claim that socialism aims to level down. The opposite is the case.

It isn't as powerful as we or indeed it thinks

Turn back now to the relative strengths and weaknesses of global capital and states. The power of global company giants can often be balanced by the power of a state.

Starbucks is a classic example inside the UK. Sales

of £3 billion produced a tax payment of £8.5 million. Faced with severe criticism, Starbucks threatened to abandon £100 million of investment and so lose 9,000 new jobs. Suppose it does not invest. Suppose it departs. That £3 billion worth of coffee and buns will still be consumed, but delivered by others who will create jobs.

Take a Scottish example, of international companies who own and control the Scotch whisky industry. How, if they do not like our tax regime, our employment laws, or that we insist bottling takes place here, not in an Asian low wage economy, will they depart with the loot? They cannot. Scotch whisky has to be made here, and nowhere else. If, however, they do take their companies elsewhere, we the people are left with the assets, and a splendid and profitable industry.

Banks are a classic example of powerful institutions with a global reach, which cannot be guaranteed survival without collective action at state level, and which can be bent to the will of a state. The socialisation of the banks in the UK and elsewhere illustrates that the community can control and influence the future of the system, if they have the will to do so.

The way manufacturing and assembly has been diced up among different countries, the reliance of pension and insurance funds on a spread of investments in various economies, and how the sheer volume of money flows in the world economy can affect currencies, are examples of the power base of international capital. A small country with an open economy such as Scotland's cannot escape from the world in which capital has such a powerful position.

There are still heights we can conquer

Nye Bevan sought to define socialism in terms of the people gaining control of the commanding heights of the economy. It would be difficult today, given the character of manufacturing and the reach that the financial services industry has, and its complexity, to identify the commanding heights that an independent Scotland could command. But there are 'important heights' that can be conquered for the public interest, and the workers' interest.

However, we must face facts. Today's socialists are confronted with the truth of limitation on what they can accomplish in terms of exerting control over many economic levers in a society. But recognising limitation does not mean accepting that nothing can be done. The combination of imagination, political willpower and what Bevan called audacity in the face of orthodoxy can make a difference in the power equation between capital and labour, and between the interests of Big capital and society.

Being realistic does not mean that socialists should not be bold, and think and act outside the boundaries that market forces wish to surround us with; nor should they be imprisoned by ideology.

This programme is bold. It shows how power can be exercised by the community, how collective action can assist people to exercise control over their individual lives. It is a programme that does not carry the weary appeals of 'hope', but instead shows how action can raise up and sustain a high level of economic activity, safeguard vital community interests, and ensure dignity for all in a country free from fear.

The Right would have us believe that the state must

shrink, and its role be confined to that of enabler: improve the supply side of the economy with laws, for example, on labour flexibility – a euphemism for fewer workers' rights and low wages. While states can be enablers in the development of an economy, they also have a dynamic role to play, can be decisive actors in key areas of the economy, and are crucial when social infrastructure is needed for the smooth running of the economic machine.

A successful society has to strike a balance between being one in which we are genuinely all in it together, and one in which the competitive edge necessary to make our national way in the business world is not diminished. A small country, egalitarian in its character, yet with a record of inventiveness, can accomplish that task. But it cannot do so when tied hand and foot to another much larger one, which does not share its political culture. Ending the deadly London connection, as that old Scottish miner advised, is a necessary start.

Striking the Right Priorities

There can be no future oil fund, when reducing the national debt is such a pressing need, in order that we can shift resources to the priority: well paid jobs.

Some 592,000 people, 21.8% of Scottish taxpayers, earn only £10,000 a year; 498,000, 18.3% earn £15,000. That picture of a low wage economy is what we have to alter.

The root issue for an independent Scottish Government is how to create growth that will create those well paid jobs, when faced with needing to pay down a large inherited debt as our share of what UK governments have created. Every £1 billion reduction in the national debt releases financial resources to stimulate growth. This programme sets out how this will be done.

The size of the national debt legacy will depend upon the skill of Scots negotiators. The blatant deception about the true value of oil, as admitted by the notorious secret Gavin McCrone memorandum, and how the £279 billion of Scotland's wealth was squandered as our nation became poorer must be taken into account in assessing the share we will take.

It is clear, however, that whether on a strict proportionate basis or a discounted share, Scotland will inherit a large national debt. As the first call upon the independence budgets will be payment of debt interest, it is imperative to get it down to levels which do not impinge destructively on a reconstruction programme.

There will be no oil future fund. There is no point paying high debt interest, when a proportion of oil wealth can be used to rapidly write down the debt, thus enabling an immediate start to creating a different economic model, and so meet the objectives of jobs, and raising living standards.

We are urged to become frightened by the fact that oil prices fluctuate, 'volatile' is the favourite description, with the dire forecast that they will go down. The Office of Budget Responsibility is the culprit. It has a wonderful title, redolent of the kind of respectability that makes people blindly accept its statements as gospel truth. Yet its record of forecasting growth is abysmal. However, the OBR gospel says oil prices will fall, and everyone cites the OBR as authority, and so it becomes legend. There will be no equivalent in a

socialist government. Budget responsibility is a ministerial function.

*Those who would terrify us with tales of woe would have
us believe that Scotland is the only nation to discover oil and
find it a problem, not a bonus. Moreover, there is more to oil
than simply getting the taxation revenues.*

Living Successfully in a New World

For almost four hundred years, world power was
exercised by the Atlantic axis – the United States
and Europe. That epoch is over. It is a new age of
Asia/Pacific power. This has been happening as the
world has moved into a new explosive technological era, probably more dramatic in its effects than
the transformation from the agricultural economy
to the industrial revolution. The other transformation comes in the role of human capital. When the
west was king, we had significant advantage over the
rest in the level of education, management, organisational and technical skills. That advantage is no
more. Millions of educated, technologically and
managerially savvy young graduates are emerging
yearly from Asian universities. Just one institution,
the Chinese Academy of Social Sciences, has fifty
research centres covering 260 disciplines and sub-
disciplines, with 4,000 full-time researchers.

As Mark Leonard points out in *What Does China
Think?*, all of the British think-tanks put together
number in the hundreds, Europe as a whole in the
low thousands, and in the USA some ten thousand
for all disciplines. The CASS is concerned only with

philosophy and social sciences. Other institutions, grounded in technology and engineering, produced 600,000 graduates last year, most from the top 50 Chinese universities.

States in the West face challenges they never before experienced in the world economic and political system. Hard-headed analysis of what we must do and what we must avoid are prerequisites for success in positioning our nation in this new world.

Assessing the Nation

Practical Steps to a New Scotland: A New Socialist Economic Model

A mistake, probably a deliberate one, made by those who forecast doom and gloom for any future Scottish economy is that they see us only as a mini-breakaway model of the UK economy. The Institute of Fiscal Studies, which tarnished its reputation by the fantastic claim to be able to see 50 years ahead, assumed we would follow the same dismal path as before.

The IFS, and others, either do not understand, or do not want to understand, that what comes with independence is the chance to think well outside the box that is the UK mindset. Independence allows us to adopt *a different economic model*. We will, of course, be subject to international demand influences as we trade with our partners, but we must adopt **resource management**, as the prime driver of the economy.

At present Scotland sits within a demand

management economy, where growth comes from consumer spending creating demand for goods and services. This requires people to borrow to spend when, as now, and for some years, wages have shrunk in real terms. It also requires government borrowing to spend on public services, because the catastrophic loss of manufacturing has unbalanced the economy. The UK government borrowing is now around £120 billion a year, accumulating towards £1.5 trillion. We are now paying the price of a one-club policy. That is why Scotland must change to build on our resources.

Resource management lies in the identification of indigenous assets from which products and services can be created to trade internally and internationally.

Scotland is rich in indigenous assets:-

1. Its people
2. Education system
3. Potential in energy generation
4. Land and agriculture
5. Fisheries
6. Oil & gas
7. Water
8. The cities
9. Scenery
10. Topography
11. Geography
12. Heritage

Tourism: the bottom five are a resource for expanding tourism, which is actually an 'export' in situ, built upon our culture, history, scenery, facilities and services. It has not met its full potential in creating jobs. Some of what is offered to tourists is good, in some cases superb. In too many places it is patchy. No product can be 'exported' that is patchy. It has to be good all over. A policy directed at aid to upgrading hotels in the 2-3 star range and the B&B sector, greater emphasis on the professional training of staff, and the policy outlined below on fuel duty, and air passenger duty, will see this industry make a greater contribution to growth and jobs.

Financial services: This is where people count. The failures at RBS and HBOS were damaging to our reputation for prudent and sound financial management. If Scotland had been alone in the arena of failure, the damage might have been irreparable. But we were not. Over 200 banks collapsed in the United States, and even Germany had to engage in bail-outs. Scotland is no more damaged than elsewhere.

There remains the considerable size of financial services, and Scotland still ranks high in the European league for funds under management. Enhancing the education and skill levels of our people will keep us in that top group.

People: Scotland has 5 million in a world of 7 billion. Disraeli's dictum: 'Upon the education of the people of this country the fate of this country depends' applies, in spades, to a small nation in a global economy.

It is imperative that Scots are educated to the highest standard in world terms in order that they position themselves to successfully ride the technological waves that will break over all economies in the years ahead. For 5 million people to earn a good living they have to perform better than most. A successful, prosperous people and a world class education system are inseparable.

Scotland's size is an advantage. The distance between policymakers and those affected is short. As in Denmark, Sweden, Finland, Norway, success or problems in policies can be quickly spotted, and action taken to either tackle failure or maximize success. That advantage is not open to larger countries. The analogy is with ships: a large tanker takes a long time to turn, a small ship can do so quickly.

Other People: Immigration. We can add to the rich resource of people with an immigration policy that suits our circumstances. Small in numbers we are, and we could gain advantages by being a bit bigger in population with the entry of people with academic qualifications, and people with a set of skills who wish to settle here permanently.

Our universities are a case in point: in a global community, they must be able to attract world-class staff from various countries and disciplines, and must be able to admit foreign students both for the fees they bring and the contribution they make to our intellectual development. Foreign students bring in over £600 million to the economy. University doors must always be wide open to foreign students and foreign academics.

Scotland must always offer asylum, but there is a difference between asylum-seeker and economic migrant. As well as university students for whom special immigration rules will apply, we should be willing to welcome others who will contribute to our economic growth and creation of wealth.

There is a moral question to be asked about economic immigration. There is a difference between admitting a migrant who lands at our door, and going out to attract and recruit a migrant. Is it right for a developed country to deliberately take from a less developed country, or one of the developing countries, their best talent? If, for example, we take doctors and nurses from a developing country, or its brightest IT-skilled young people, does that not seriously hamper the chances of advancement for the countries from which they come?

What we need is a sensible immigration policy that is not self-centred while seeking to attract people of talent. People who leave their countries in search of betterment for themselves and their children and undertake dangerous journeys have the kind of character and innate ability, the 'fresh talent', that can be built upon by countries in which they arrive. Scotland should have a quota system for economic migrants irrespective of colour or creed, and should have specific policies and mechanisms for them and their children, to become established and integrated into our communities as new Scots.

This need for induction into Scotland and its values and laws is not a minor matter. Some, not all, immigrant cultural norms are unacceptable here. The subordinate role of women, 'honour' killings and the abhorrent practice of female genital mutilation have no place in a Scotland where the advances in rights, especially women's rights, is not an accident, but the product of years, decades, of struggle by progressive forces.

Education, Education, Education

Blair said it. This programme means it. Education is the foundation of a successful society, both in terms of economic and social achievements at home and an ability to participate constructively in the international community.

It is time to end the foolish claims that we have a world-class education system. This nation has gone from being able to boast of a fully literate population to one where many have difficulty in reading, writing and counting, and our universities are faced with first-year students who have no grammar and cannot spell, or write with precision.

We rightly boast of five universities in the world's top two hundred ... but our universities have the worst drop-out rate in the UK ... and, to our everlasting shame, we have children born to fail at school, not because teachers are incompetent or uncaring, but because the social conditions in certain localities impose limits on the children's horizons and kill ambition at an early age. The correlation between the numbers of free school meals and low exam performance tells its own story. Apart from being morally repugnant, that failure is economically damaging. To lift this nation to a position where it can be successful, we need to start with the children. The replacement of the selection system by comprehensive schools in the 1960s has been a success in many areas where there has been a balance in the social mix of students. But it is not perfect or near to world class, and it is time this was admitted and new ideas allowed to flow in.

A New Education Act

Purpose: To ensure no child is born to fail. All Scottish school students will be equipped to succeed in the world

The new Act will give effect to the restructuring of higher education, creation of local authority Joint Education Boards, release of more money direct to schools, head teachers with greater autonomy over school budgets and recruitment, and the direction of exceptional assistance to schools in designated areas of multiple deprivation.

The aim of the Act is that every child will develop the skills to think critically in maths, science and reading, learn to solve problems that will enable them to adapt, and take advantage of, and not be overwhelmed by, the further technological changes that will come as this century unfolds. Knowledge is going to matter more in this century than in any previous one. This policy embraces every child from birth. No country either economically or morally can accept a situation where in certain areas, children fail who, in any other social environment, would succeed. The present set-up fails them. It must be changed.

The Ministry of Education will define and designate areas of multiple deprivation for the purposes of the Act. Primary and secondary schools in these areas will receive double the per capita allocation. Schools in these areas are faced with external social factors that seriously impinge upon their ability to engage pupils and students in the imperative of learning. A teacher's role is in the classroom, yet if he or she is to properly educate children and students, the external social conditions must be tackled. To this end each secondary school will have a non-education 'Social & Community Development' department whose job it will be to work with families in the area, to build capacity for self-improvement where that is required, and engender greater parental interest and involvement in the children and the school.

School buildings and facilities will be made available to the 'Social & Community Development' department after schools hours, at weekends and during school holiday periods for their work in the community. The Workers Educational Association should be engaged in activities designed to improve the education levels of parents through specialised courses.

The work of **Sistema Scotland** in creating the Big Noise orchestras in Raploch and Govanhill will be helped in a way that sustains its expansion without interference in its voluntary nature. The Scottish Government, to its credit, made £1.5 million available to Sistema and commissioned research on the impact that its work has had on families, children and communities. As the research noted, there were significant improvements in the confidence, self-esteem, social skills and ability to concentrate among the children in the Raploch orchestra. Music can transform. Philanthropists will be encouraged to continue, and new ones to join in doing so, by a policy that provides £3 from the Scottish Government for £1 given. Whatever the outcome of that policy, Sistema will be guaranteed no less a sum than £3 million per year for its work with no government strings attached.

Schools outwith the designated deprived areas will also make their buildings available for educational, social and recreational use as a matter of national policy. Many do so already. This policy has implications.

State Schools will get Charitable Status

It is difficult to see how the type of state school, with its additional social and community development commitment, or a more open attitude to its use by the community, differs from a school in the independent sector in terms of qualification for charitable status. The only factor which disqualifies state schools from charitable status, because they definitely pass the test of 'public benefit' set by the Charities & Trustee Investment (Scotland) Act 2005, is that they are construed as being under the direction or control of Ministers. Even if they are, they far outstrip the independent schools in terms of delivering a public benefit.

It seems absurd that the independent sector should get the charitable status denied to state schools, when both pass the test set by the Act. The new Education Act will be accompanied legislatively with amendments to the 2005 Charities Act, to remove the obstruction of Ministerial involvement. It may be true that Ministers supply funding for state schools, but by no means do they exercise detailed direction or control over individual schools, the responsibility for which lies with local authorities. The issue of charitable status is no small matter.

Paul Hutcheon, *Sunday Herald*, 22 July 2012, revealed:-

> Fettes, because of the 80% discount as a charity, saw its council tax liability fall from £209,139 to £41,828. George Watson's College fell from £412,649 to £83,530, Gordonstoun's from £148,086 to 30,618. Wester Hailes state school,

having no such status, where 45% of pupils were eligible for free school meals, paid its full liability of £261,873.

The same 80% reduction in council tax (LVT when introduced) will apply to all state schools.

Educating the Young

The Present Structure is Faulty, and Will Be Made Right

At the heart of this education policy lie four priorities:
>Ensuring that never again will a Scottish child be born to fail
>Enhancing the status and quality of the teaching profession
>Allocation of funding for universities to keep our sciences world class
>Ensuring that investment in tertiary education will, in progressive steps, reach the level of 2.8 % of GDP

The Under Fives

The crucial age group

Research has proved that if a child is badly treated or ignored, or is not stimulated in its early years, then it is loaded with difficulties in future years. Lesley Riddoch, who has done a great deal of study in this area of child development, quoted in *The Scotsman* (18 November 2013), research showing that 'By age five, children with a degree-educated parent are, on average, 18 months ahead in their vocabulary ability compared with children whose parents have no qualifications. They are 13 months ahead in problem-solving abilities.'

She points out that before 2003 'health visitors used to make universal checks at six weeks, three months, eight months, 18 months, two years, 3.3 years and just before school.' Those health checks were reduced by the Labour/Lib Dem administration.

As there is a direct correlation between what happens to the general health and development of a child under five, and performance at the various levels of schools, each nursery and primary school will have a health care unit whose function will be to work with families in communities scarred by deprivation, and the full universal checks will be restored. This means more health visitors, an increase of 20 per cent. This will cost, but if the programme is serious about the importance of education for the nation and for the individual, the cost will be met.

Money spent in the nurturing and development of Scotland's children is money well spent. There is a terrible legacy from the destructive years of the Thatcher government. The children today and those born in the future bear no responsibility for the situation many families are in. They are entitled to live in a society that is different from one where so many are mired in poverty. If boldness is required to give them the priority, then let us be bold.

Kindergartens & Nursery Schools: A full-time, all-day place for every child between the ages of 1 & 5 in deprived areas, and between 3 and 5 elsewhere. These will be staffed not only with trained nursery teachers and health specialists, as set out above, but also with social support staff for single mothers and other families. There will be after-school care provided.

Part of the money released by the amalgamation of education authorities will contribute towards the cost of a place for every child.

Teachers

The status of the teachers must be raised to that of an elite profession. This will mean higher standards of entry and continuing professional development. It will mean higher salaries. As a benchmark, no Principal teacher will be paid less than £50,000 a year, and no experienced teacher less than £40,000 per year.

There is no doubt that class size matters, but it is the quality of the teaching that counts most. A *teacher who can inspire a child to seek knowledge, impart a thirst for learning, enable a child to recognise and appreciate its own talent and ability, and so build its sense of self worth, and ignite ambition, is an asset to be cherished and rewarded.*

Restructuring the Education System

If Universities and Further Education Colleges are to flourish and contribute significantly to Scottish success in a wide range of fields of endeavour, they must be presented with students who are exceptionally well educated, have a thirst for knowledge, and prize education for the great gift it is.

Whether universities and further education colleges flourish is wholly dependent upon the rock of our education system – nursery, primary and secondary schooling. It is in these that social disadvantage must be tackled. It isn't simply having more financial resources allocated, but how resources are used.

Right now, with 32 educational authorities, administration absorbs too much of the money allocated to schools.

In their place will be five local authority Joint Education Boards: Strathclyde, Dumfries & Galloway, Edinburgh & Lothians, Forth, Fife & Tayside, Highlands Islands & Grampian. The voting membership will be elected councillors from each council in the joint board area, plus one non-voting advisor from each of the Universities and Higher Technical Institutes in the area. This reduces administration, with substantial savings, enabling more money to be channelled to where it should go – the schools. A reduction of education authorities from 32 to 5, would, it is estimated, release some £400-500 million. This format retains the role of elected local councillors, and adds expertise and advice from educational organisations that are dependent upon the primary and secondary schools systems for students who are well educated.

Joint Boards will receive direct funding from the Ministry of Education, thus ensuring the money is ringfenced. Joint Boards will allocate to schools. When receiving their budgets, Head Teachers will have greater autonomy over how money is spent on staffing, recruitment, materials and support services.

There will be no selection. The comprehensive system will continue to apply as national policy, as will the curriculum for excellence. In 1965, before the introduction of comprehensive education with its social mix, 70% left secondary school without nationally recognised qualifications. Only 12% of school leavers qualified for higher education. Three decades later only one in twenty five young people left school without a qualification. In 2011-12, 36.8% earned three or more Highers.

But there is this problem of schools in areas where there is virtually no social mix, where social stress and deprivation is the norm, where children are born to fail and where upward social mobility is not even a dream.

Concern for this lack of social mobility prompted the Rector of Kelvinside Academy, in a letter to *The Herald*, 21 November 2013, to advocate vouchers so that 'children from all sections of society' would gain greater access to leading schools, including the independents, provided the government 'help fund places for children in the best schools.' What that would entail is turning our state schools into a marketplace, competing with each other for students, and where demand for a school outstripped places, the reintroduction of selection. What the advocates of selection seem blind to is that the unselected are damaged by that process. If only *x* number of places are available, the exclusion of children who do not get in, although they may be very bright, is not only unfair but a criminal waste. A sense of failure for the majority not selected was the marked feature of the pre-1965 system. There will be no return to that.

But, there are schools where there is little or no social mix, where the children are drawn from areas of social stress which make it extremely difficult for teachers to imbue them with self-confidence and a desire for education. Vouchers will not change those children's prospects, only resources properly applied will improve their chances in life.

It is to find resources, in addition to those reallocated from administrative savings, that PFI/PPP agreements must be renegotiated. Between 2013-14 and 2041-42, the Scottish public sector will pay over £24.346 billion. Taken to the cleaners is a phrase that comes to mind. How to handle PFI/PPP providers if they are reluctant to renegotiate is set out later in the section dealing with the NHS.

Primary and Secondary schools

Primary. Pilot schemes in England have shown that children who have access to free meals at school find it not only good for physical development, but good for educational attainment. Free school meals will be available in primary schools from P1 to P7.

Secondary. In the state secondary schools there will be a marked shift, so that while those of an academic bent will continue as at present, other students will, from end S3 onwards, be engaged in developing technical/vocational skills along with academic studies – thus meeting the need not met at present, that is giving a group of young people a chance to accumulate skills that will engage their interest, and open up to them work opportunities in the years after school.

At the end of S3, students who do not wish to

continue in the academic stream will transfer to Higher Technical Institutes (former FE colleges) for the rest of their education, with that education having a heavy technical bent. These institutes will offer a triple quality to students transferring from school: their status, professional lecturers, and their awards. They represent another different, but equal, step along the educational road.

Those young people taking up Higher Technical Institute courses will benefit from the policy of full employment pursued by a socialist government. The constant striving by that government to achieve and maintain that policy will alter perceptions among the young.

There is a crucial link between education and jobs. Part of the problem in deprived areas is that young people at school see no prospect of a job, and so any attempt to persuade them that education is important for their future life chances is likely to fall on deaf ears. If they lived in a country where job availability was the norm, then approaches to what education has to offer would be different.

Enhancing the Status of the FE Sector

Higher Technical Institutes

If Further Education Colleges are to improve the contribution they make to education in general, their status in the eyes of students must rise, not as a PR exercise, but because they gift each one significant and worthwhile levels of knowledge, skills and qualifications. This objective can only be met through direct funding from the Ministry of Education, with advisory boards drawn from the local community, including business. Close relations with Lead Boards from industry will ensure that each sector maintains a high technical standard and a skill set that recognises the importance of literacy, numeracy and citizenship.

FE Colleges will become Higher Technical Institutes awarding Technical Baccalaureates. Staffing structure will be reorganised to reflect their higher status and the role they will play with students.

Higher Technical Institutes will be seen as a first choice for those who wish to excel in technical and vocational skills. The Technical Baccalaureates and the Technical Baccalaureate Diploma will set benchmarks against which intellectual, creative and vocational skillsets will be measured and recognised. Both Baccalaureates will aim at excellence, a 'Gold' standard of education, lacking in the present competence based system. The Technical Baccalaureate will also allow credit transfer to the University sector for students who, under this new system, are able and willing to pursue their studies further.

A crucial aspect of this new policy is that a broad range of local and national economic indicators will act as the key drivers for course development, and the measure of course viability will be part of broader aspirations than being driven by local market demand. This will allow access to specific courses where local numbers may be low, but the benefit to the local or national community is high.

The University Sector

Against elitism, are we?

Nothing more illustrates the perversion that exists within the current philosophy (*sic*) in higher education than the peculiar idea that our universities, which are truly in a global market place, should deny entry to those academically qualified, while admitting students with lesser qualifications because they come from a deprived socio-economic strata. This is well intentioned, done in the interests of those whose start in life, and whose travel through the education system is difficult, when compared with others. It is an expensive gesture, not in financial terms, but in terms of erosion in the long term of the academic worth of our university system.

That Scotland should have a high student dropout rate is not surprising. Young people from deprived areas, especially if they have lower academic standards than their peer group, are going to suffer problems of confidence in what is a very different academic and social environment, where the demands are on an ability to engage in autonomous learning. They are in at the deep end with very little background to support them.

It is, again, peculiar that while in the armed forces our society admires the elite units, and we long for the day when an elite squad will emerge to form our national football team, when we enjoy seeing Scots become part of the acting elite of Holywood, and rejoice in the elite status of Andy Murray, we look disdainfully at any notion of elitism in our education system at university level.

Socialists must argue that every young person, no matter their background, should reach the highest level of educational placement and attainment to which they are capable. If we are to carve out a national economic life in a global world, we need to ensure that our elite universities should take in only the highest qualified. To ensure that no student is put off by the threat of debt, the policy of free tuition will continue.

Making Scotland the outstanding Scientific Centre in Europe

Scotland already has world class universities in the area of science. The policy will be to build upon that and make us the leading science centre in Europe. The anxiety expressed about scientific research after leaving the UK is not about our universities' research capabilities, but funding. The sum involved is around £330 million a year.

The Ministry of Education will have two funds for universities. One, the general fund drawn from government taxation revenues, will be distributed by the Higher Education Funding Council as of now, thus guaranteeing that the humanities are given their due weight. The second fund, also to be distributed by HEFC, will be dedicated to science research disciplines in which our universities are world class, or where the potential is there to reach that standard.

This second fund will be ring-fenced. It will substitute for the research funding presently obtained from UK sources, which amount to £330 million per year. The fund will be created by selling Scotland's shares in RBS and Lloyds banks to which we are entitled. These shares total around £42 billion, and Scotland's share will release £3-4 billion to plug the research gap while a new income stream is created by involvement in the Scottish National Oil Corporation (set out later).

It is on this base of world excellence that Scotland can become an even more outstanding centre for research and development in science. The universities which get funding will be charged with ensuring that as well as working with large, international companies, they will seek to enhance, through research, the performance of SMEs in the science and engineering sectors.

The Need for Universities to Balance Research with Teaching

Notwithstanding the importance of scientific research, as a general principle applicable to all subjects, there has to be a better balance between the role of the university as a teacher of students and as a resource for research. The present pressure for research as the decisive factor in funding is downgrading teaching. This is a legacy from the Thatcher years. Research is important, but, as *The Times* pointed out last November in a leader, so is the teaching of students, the generation after generation who must leave with the intellectual capacity to understand and respond to the challenges produced by a world still in the infancy of the technological revolution. Our society needs to rediscover a reverence for knowledge for its own sake. Our universities need to rediscover a mission to spread knowledge widely throughout society.

Universities should not be used as social engineering mechanisms, or training schools for what business says it requires, but are, or should be, seats of learning and teaching. The restoration of that role is essential to creating a society capable of understanding the world in which we must live, and to having the lateral thinking and broad minds we need to respond successfully to the challenges and problems we will face.

A Pre-University College

For young people from the deprived areas, with the minimum of required Highers, who are now admitted to universities as part of the 'equality' policy, and who have a high chance of dropping out with devastating consequences for their self-worth, there will be a year-long course at a pre-university campus institution, where they can experience the transition to higher education, consolidate their academic achievements, and find their feet in an entirely different social environment, thus enabling them to enter the university that has offered a place, with a year of valuable experience already under their belts. They will be fully funded in that year by a grant.

This institution will have very high standards and be run by a dedicated staff and principal drawn from the academic community, with links to the Open University Scotland which has an excellent record of teaching people from a variety of backgrounds.

Jobs, Jobs, Jobs

Those who think we should accept a pool of
unemployment, should try swimming in it.

Jobs. There are two ways to cut the welfare budget and
release the money spent on it for other, productive purposes. **The Tory way** is to cut the benefits of the poor.
Thatcher's government (lauded by Cameron) saw the
destruction of jobs in communities, and now the victims, the under twenty-fives in particular have become
the villains, as though they bear the guilt of economic
problems and must be punished.

A single mother and her child, because the former is
under the age of 25, is singled out as undeserving if she
does not work. Meantime, Alex Fergusson MSP, former
Presiding Officer of the Scottish Parliament, will be in
receipt of £40,000 a year gotten, not by the sweat of
his brow, but because he owns land upon which stand
wind Turbines. He is not alone. The Earl of Glasgow
will receive £210,000 per annum, the Earl of Seafield
£120,000, the Earl of Moray £300,000 and Sir Alastair
Gordon-Cumming £435,000. These payments will be
made over the 25-year lifetime of the wind turbines.
A generous subsidy is paid by, among others, a single
mother through her high cost energy bills. This benefit seems to draw no criticism. To those that have will
be given is not a principle to be tolerated in a socialist Scotland. Changes to landownership and use (see
below) will deal with this unearned income.

The socialist way, the best way, is to create well-paid
jobs in a drive for full employment. A pipedream will

say the sceptics. Yet, the opposite of full employment is high unemployment. The Bank of England benchmark is 7%. That represents an enormous number of Scots permanently on the dole. That level of unemployment renders workers vulnerable to low wages and wage cuts. It need not be like that.

Economic policy does not come from God sending it down like punitive bolts from cosmic space, well beyond our control to resist. It comes from policies made by human beings, and so other human beings can alter and reverse that policy. There are a number of ways of creating real jobs to give people work if a state is transformed from a neutral to a dynamic driver.

'Work' crying out to be done

Look around any part of Scotland and you will see work crying out to be done. Take the deterioration of our tenement housing stock, where not only the walls but the roofs and closes need big repairs and upgrading. It is a long time ago that any programme of upgrading took place in our cities. Where community housing associations exist, the organisational and financial capabilities are there to tackle the 'work' needing to be done. Where the properties are in owner-occupier hands, it is a different matter – the deterioration continues. The funding of tenement improvements by central government 95% grants, with the balance drawn from the owners, would be a big stimulus to small private builders, and provide them with a sufficient volume of work to take on apprentices.

Here is another example: we are told there must be a legacy from the Olympics and the Commonwealth

Games. There is to be a super facility for elite athletes so that Scots can compete in future international events. Again no problem with selective elitism. But the number of elite is small. What about the rest who enjoy sports, and will benefit from better facilities?

There are a number of excellent sports facilities available, but by no means everywhere, especially in the small towns where athletics clubs exist, but without good facilities, and in some cases none. That is 'work' crying out to be done.

There are many other examples that could be given: community facilities in villages and small towns that have not been upgraded for years, land that is an eyesore in cities and towns, small flood prevention schemes vital to a few families but not big enough to be a local authority priority. We have communities that now own their land, and there is work needed to improve it. There are islands that would benefit from enhancement of the physical environment to attract tourism.

Scottish Environmental Engineering Corps

All of the above, and more, can be tackled by a new organisation, The Scottish Environmental Engineering Corps, modelled on the United States Army Corps of Engineers. That organisation, anchored in the disciplinary framework of the US army, has a remit to provide vital public engineering and design services to strengthen construction management, undertake specific beneficial projects, and energise the economy. Just what Scotland needs.

On independence we will have a Scottish defence force. It will have people with considerable experience in organisation, logistics and management, combined with a wide range of technical and engineering skills, a history of recruiting in areas where the young have had serious disadvantages, and turning them, through its structures, into able young adults.

The SEEC will part of the defence force. It will consist of regular SDF personnel, a cohort of civilian engineers and architects, and young people recruited from the areas of deprivation. In total it will be 15,000 strong.

SEEC will carry out civic works for communities, giving its young recruits the experience of skilled work at proper apprenticeship and journeyman levels, in what they require – a life that is structured and disciplined, and above all rewarding both in money wages earned and self-esteem.

Revenue and funding for the SEEC and its projects will come from the regular defence force budget.

Housing Development Authority

Scotland has 157,000 families on the waiting list for social housing. Waiting lists show just how short is the supply to meet this demand. In Glasgow the waiting list is 40,000, North Lanarkshire 15,905, Dundee 5,846, Edinburgh 25,548.

The negative effect upon children and their education when living in poor housing conditions is a factor that cannot be overlooked when deciding that housing the people is a priority.

Housing the people requires 25,000 new build social houses per year for ten years. Thirty-two local councils is a fractured structure, quite unable to meet the logistical and build-capacity this emergency demands.

That need is for an organisation with power to acquire land and employ the manpower to build in partnership with the private construction sector on that land, and has the legal ability to by-pass local bureaucracy and the managerial capacity to allocate new housing fairly and collect the rents as a landlord.

The Housing Development Authority is the answer. Initial revenue for the first two years funded by central government, and capital for building and future revenue until rentals flow, raised through housing development bonds with the housing stock and rental income standing as collateral. AAA stuff. These bonds are ideal for Islamic finance as the 'sukuk' involves investment that engages risk with the right to profit from success.

Action by the Housing Development Authority will be a significant stimulus to the construction industry and its supply chain, creating thousands of jobs and real apprenticeships.

Scottish Hospital Ship and International Rescue Service

Scottish Overseas Service

When this policy was discussed with some colleagues, many, not all, expressed the view that it would invite mockery and so prejudice any objective assessment of the other policies. That is a risk, but one taken for the purpose of refocusing what power we have from killing people to healing them. The idea was first mentioned by me at a Yes meeting in Edinburgh more than a year ago. The disaster in the Philippines and the role of aircraft carriers in rescue operations underline its good sense.

For more generations than is comfortable to recall, Scottish servicemen have been at the forefront of the UK's projection of hard power. It was necessary in the 1939-45 war against Fascism, but before that it was often to advance or defend British imperialism. The sentimentality exhibited at any threat to the Scottish Regiments shows the Scottish mind still engaged with the idea of hard power. The new independent Scotland, if it wants to be influential in the international community, should be projecting soft power. Power that delivers humanitarian aid is preferable to power that delivers a bullet from a gun.

Juxtaposed to that military tendency, there is a broad streak of idealism in the Scottish people, which makes them ready to respond to those in need or danger across the world. This policy gives expression to that tradition; it tells the world that we are committed to helping and healing and that we can take a weapon originally intended for war, and turn it into an instrument that is wholly peaceful. The policy is idealism in practice. If not swords into ploughshares, then a war ship into a peace ship.

The Government in London has two aircraft carriers under construction. The Royal Navy needs only one. What to do with the other? Either it will be mothballed, or sold at an enormous discount to a foreign navy. As there has to be a division of assets upon independence, the new Scottish Government will take it. Not to equip is as a warship, but as an effective platform for the new Scottish Hospital and International Rescue Service, to deliver vital medical aid where there is none available to people, and humanitarian aid when natural disasters strike.

The Scottish Overseas Service (SOS) will be open to young people from the age of sixteen to twenty drawn from right across the social strata. There will places for two hundred every year in the hospital ships. They will contribute to the work, and their experience of aiding people in poor conditions or acute distress will enable them to reach a better understanding of the issues that have to be tackled by us all in this world of humanity.

The Robert Burns

The converted aircraft carrier, The Robert Burns, will be modelled on the *Africa Mercy* Hospital Ship, but will provide medical care on a far larger scale. It will have a dual role. Its primary one will be to act as a hospital ship visiting areas in Africa and Asia, providing medical care for the poorest people, together with training for local healthcare workers.

The *Africa Mercy* delivers healthcare to some of the world's poorest people, deprived of decent health services. This ship (16,500 tons) has five operating theatres, an 82-bed recovery ward, CT scanner, X-ray machines and a laboratory. It treats a wide range of problems including cleft lip and palate, cataract, burns, burns scars, general surgery, dental care, and eye operations. In one year it performed 3,300 surgical operations, 27,800 medical and eye consultations, 2,600 eye operations, and 34,700 dental procedures. It trained 12,600 in health care. It is involved in projects such as HIV/AIDS prevention, and the construction of wells and public health improvements.

The Robert Burns will be staffed with trained doctors, dentists, nurses, auxiliaries, and be fully equipped as a hospital. It will be linked to the Scottish medical schools, and thus able to draw upon their expertise. For this role and its emergency humanitarian role, it will have a crew of around 2,500, plus the young SOS volunteers.

Its other role will be to deliver aid to areas devastated by natural disasters. For that it will have stores of tents, blankets, water, medicines, rescue machinery, and will be manned by medical personnel and skilled emergency aid-workers, and run by experienced sailors commanded by senior officers. It will fly the Saltire to represent its service to save lives.

The total personnel of the service will be around 5,000. Its headquarters and personnel accommodation will be at Faslane, where it will have relief crews and training programmes. It will be a uniformed service.

The expected annual running costs of a new carrier put into commission as a warship by the Royal Navy is £44 million (source: Navy Matters) including refits. As a Hospital ship, the running costs will be lower than that – around £35 million per year.

Funding for the service will come from the overseas aid budget. At present, Scotland contributes around £1.1 billion to the UK aid budget. This sum will be repatriated upon independence.

If this policy, as some fear, invites mockery, so be it. But those who mock should, perhaps, consider whether they have the right target. Is it not a matter for mockery that the people who have ordered this ship don't want it, and have no idea of what to do with it? What is there to mock in a policy that takes a large redundant ship, and turns it into a hospital for the poorest of the poor?

Africa and Asia are not the only parts of the world in which poor people require medical care, or help when natural disasters strike. The Caribbean is another area, with Haiti an example. A new hospital ship of 16,500 tons, similar to the Africa Mercy, will be built for work in that region, in the Clyde yards.

The Oil Industry

To miss the Oil bonus once was folly, to miss it twice would be criminal stupidity

A radical overhaul of the North Sea Oil industry can deliver a £200 billion injection to the economy over the next 20 years
Sir Ian Wood's review report

Scotland is the only developed nation where oil was discovered and grew poorer. Scots have the unique distinction of being the only nation where its discovery is seen as a problem and not a bonus. Oil wealth will flow from Scottish waters for at least the next 40 years. Knowledge about the industry and its true wealth has been locked away from the

Scots in a prison of lies. The international community know the truth.

As Martyn Tulloch and Gordon Wilson pointed out in a detailed paper, the 27th Licensing Round in 2012 produced 224 applications, the highest number ever. Initial offers for 167 production licenses were made. Twelve new companies entered the business, and twelve operators alone committed £31.5 billion to new developments. There is some £1.5 trillion of wealth still in the North Sea. So far, forty-one billion barrels have been extracted and another twenty-one billion are still to be had (source: Sir Ian Wood).

The oil and gas industry is not just a system from which fossil fuel flows. It is a resource upon which other economic activities can be built, especially in technology development, and onshore jobs could be spread more widely throughout Scotland.

A Scottish National Oil Corporation

If oil wealth is to make a significant mark upon the inherited debt, then the take from it has to be greater than what comes from taxes. To date the debate about oil has been based on the present tax take. That is not appropriate for an independent country. We have to look at the oil issue with different eyes. It is too late to do a Norway, but not too late to use sovereign power to assert the national interest in a more robust way.

There will be a new **North Sea National Interest Act**. It will create a **Scottish National Oil Corporation**. The Act will give SNOC the right to a stake of 10% in the production and profit from each company operating under licences up to the and including the 27th Round. Thereafter, in any future Round, the stake will be 15%. This is a modest call compared to the policies that operate internationally. Denmark gets a 20% stake in each new licensed project. The Corporation will hold the shares on its books.

The Higher Education Funding Council will hold 30% of the shares in SNOC, and be entitled to the dividends, thus giving them a role in the Corporation and an income stream to enhance research.

SNOC will offer 30% of its share value to Scottish institutional investors, and if they fail to take up the whole amount allocated, it will float the rest on international stock markets. SNOC will retain the balance. The Act will prevent HEFC selling its shares other than to SNOC, and the latter will be prevented from disposing of shares to the private sector beyond the 30%.

The Corporation will be run on commercial lines, and its share of distributed profit will be paid to the Scottish Government, for general policy purposes and to reduce fuel duty (see below).

In addition to acting as above, the Corporation will have the power, through the issue of oil bonds, to buy into companies operating in the North Sea, including the ability to buy one of the medium sized companies. In doing so, it will be acting no differently from any other business. Again, Islamic finance through the 'sukuk' system is an ideal method: investment with excellent prospects of return on success.

The Scottish Government cannot maximize its power over oil without there being wide knowledge about the industry among the people. Scots have little understanding of the industry compared, for example, to the general knowledge that existed in the past about ship-building, steel and mining. The new Oil Corporation will not only act as an instrument of national interest, but its existence, and reports from it, will open a 'window' to greater understanding by government and people.

The Second Bonus

Scottish North Sea Oil Directorate

In the debate over the value of Scottish oil, not enough attention has been paid to the opportunity arising from the decommissioning of rigs which, properly handled, offers a better balancing of the economy based on engineering and at advanced levels. Oil & Gas UK, the offshore industry's organisation, reports that decommissioning of rigs offers work valued at £10.3 billion over the next decade, and a total of £28.7 billion by 2040.

To ensure that Scots get their proper share of this work, a Scottish North Sea Oil Directorate will be established by law, with powers to direct oil and gas companies operating rigs in Scottish waters, which they intend to decommission, to carry out that work in designated island and mainland locations where capacity exists. Where additional capacity is needed the Scottish Government will assist the private sector in creating it, and will provide training grants to ensure there is a workforce able to undertake this work.

Public Utilities

That utilities essential to individual lives and the national economy, like electricity, gas, railways, airports and postal services, should be in foreign ownership raises questions about a possible conflict between their commercial interests and the national interest.

As these private companies obtained their positions legitimately in law, and as the rule of law has to be respected in a parliamentary democracy, we cannot confiscate their property, nor is there any prospect on cost grounds alone for wholesale nationalisation. That does not mean that an independent Scotland must endure the status quo – the legacy of Thatcherism from our days as an impotent part of the UK. There are things that can be done to protect the public interest.

New laws which, whilst not removing the utility companies' rights of ownership, can modify their power.

Airports and Aviation

With the exception of Prestwick, Inverness, Dundee and outlying islands, Scotland's major airports at Aberdeen, Edinburgh and Glasgow are in private hands. These latter three in particular are a strategic resource whose management and development is crucial to economic success. A socialist government could not possibly allow them to make decisions about development only in the interests of the companies who own them.

Glasgow and Aberdeen are owned by the company that owns Heathrow, and that company in turn is owned by a consortium in which Qatar, Singapore and China have substantial shareholdings. Global Infrastructure Partner, a transnational, owns Edinburgh along with Gatwick and London City. The two companies, it will be noted, have a commercial interest in feeding passengers from Aberdeen, Edinburgh and Glasgow into their London assets for long haul flights. A marked feature of Scotland is the relatively few long-haul flights from the two central Scotland airports.

It is not only passengers affected by the lack of long-haul flights. As Iain Lawson has pointed out in a paper for Options for Scotland: 'Air cargo is also an important consideration ... Scotland is particularly weak in this area due to the lack of European and Worldwide destinations .... Recent figures showed that while Scotland exported around £500 million worth of whisky last year, England exported over **£2.4 billion** of whisky as most of it left from ports and airports' located there.

It is a fair question to ask, given the weight of the London airports in the portfolio of the owners of Glasgow, Aberdeen and Edinburgh, whether there is within those companies the kind of imperative to gain the long-haul direct flights that Scotland's tourist and other businesses need in an age when air travel is so vital. These are big companies, money is not available to buy into them to the extent of gaining access as of right at board level, or of a takeover.

Given that independence gifts a Scottish Government with power over aviation policy, a socialist answer to how the public interest is inserted, within the limits above, is to impose licence conditions for their continued operation. The licence would set out conditions which would include policies to prioritise the securing of more direct long-haul destinations. *It is important to recognise that airports are run as purely commercial undertakings when, in fact, they are a public service and a tool of economic policy.*

This is no small matter. The informative paper by Iain Lawson shows that '50% of foreign holiday visitors to Scotland travel no further than Glasgow and Edinburgh ... as they need to return south to catch their return flights.' According to Visit Scotland overseas tourism accounts for 35% of total tourist spend. There should be, and would be, more tourists if direct flights were available. As it is, for example, the majority of US visitors land in England and never leave it, because of the extra expense in coming up here.

Air Passenger Duty

Westminster policy on APD sees band A (0-2000 miles) rise to £26 from April, band B (2001-4000 miles) to £138, and Band C to £170 (4001-6000 miles).

APD will be abolished. At first sight that policy would appear to reduce the Scottish government's revenues by £230 million, but not necessarily so. PwC research published in February 2013 found that cutting or abolishing APD would result a) in a significant increase in UK GDP and b) in an increase in revenues for the treasury from other taxes as a result of economic stimulus – actually paying for itself.

Abolition in Scotland should assist the tourist industry and business. However, although this will help direct short-haul and some direct long-haul passengers flying from Scottish airports, it will not relieve Scots from APD completely, as they will be charged by the

Westminster government if feeding into London for long-haul flights to, for example, China.

As revealed by the PwC research, getting more direct long-haul flights from areas we draw upon for tourism, and for our business travellers seeking new markets in Asia, is a critical issue lying at the heart of Scottish aviation policy.

Fuel Duty

The present level of fuel duty is a burden on business and a drag on growth. That is especially so in a country like Scotland with sparse population areas in the Highlands, and a number of island communities. Fuel duty will be cut. That will help growth in general, and be of substantial assistance to the tourist industry.

Policy on fuel duty at UK level cannot, and does not, take account of Scotland's geography. UK policy has been punitive, one of its ironic features being that the nearer one gets to the oil fields, the dearer petrol becomes.

Fuel duty comes in two forms – a straight tax of 57.9p and VAT at 22.215p per litre, making a total tax of 80.1p, bringing a litre, once other real costs are factored in, to 132.9p.

Fuel duty reduction will be from 57.9p to 42p per litre. That will bring the total cost per litre to:-

Duty	42p
Product	47.8p
Retail	5p
	94.8p
VAT 18%	17.06
Total	**111.86p (a reduction of 21.06p per litre).**

Electricity & Gas Companies

There are three ways to assert the public interest: changes to shareholding, corporate governance, and how companies sell their products.

Shares and corporate governance. Regulators, tough ones, have an important role in guarding the public interest. We need to reinforce that interest. A new Energy Law will come into force within six months of independence. This will enable the Scottish Government to take a 15% stake in the shares of electricity and gas companies, and nominate a 'public interest director' to each company board. The new Act will alter company law. All directors will have a duty to the public interest, and this will come before any duty to shareholders.

The products. What the population needs, especially the elderly and sick, is guaranteed heat in their homes at prices they can afford. Business too cannot afford to be ripped off.

The new law will require two levels of charges, a basic one at reasonable cost to the consumers, set by the Regulator, with calculations based on a lower rate of return than the companies seek at present, and a higher one, also set by the Regulator, where a higher return can be agreed. The Regulator will ensure that the basic charge enables low income households to avoid a choice between heating and eating.

The ideal would be to take these companies into public ownership, but there are other areas where the use of financial instruments is of a higher priority. The treble whammy of Regulator, shareholding and public interest assertion at board level should bring their operations nearer to what is required. Objective judgment of the policy will reveal that it is quite radical.

The negotiations on the basic charge will be complicated by the existence of the wind and wave energy projects, constantly extolled as the great way forward by scottish ministers, but which impose considerable costs in their present stage of development.

Resource Management of Renewables & Fracking

Present energy policy is an expensive mess. It is logical to subsidise an infant industry to get it on its feet, but how long the infancy and how well households and business are able to pay the subsidy is the matter on which judgment is required.

Anxiety about climate change, stoked by lobby groups with a vested interest, has meant little critical analysis of the claims for renewables by the people who pay the subsidies – the consumers – confronted as they are by a barrage of propaganda and acronyms that create confusion about the true nature of the issues and consequences. One of the tricks when giving information on wind turbines is to cite capacity 'able to light so many thousands of homes.' But as wind turbines can only produce around 28% of capacity because the wind either doesn't blow or blows too hard for the turbines to operate, lots of those homes would in reality be in the dark.

Wind and wave power are free, but turning them into electricity and delivering it to households and business is far from free. Whereas wholesale energy is priced from conventional sources at £50/MWh, onshore wind is £94/MWh and off-shore wind rise to £140-180 MWh. Wave and tidal come in at £350-400MWh and £200-300 MWh respectively (source Dept. Energy & Climate Change).

Targets of 100% national production through renewables requires large sustained subsidies, extremely expensive electricity, with serious implications for households and businesses who have to shoulder the financial burden. The people cannot afford those costs, and neither can business which, faced with the highest green costs compared to eleven major industrial countries, will lose competitiveness and shed jobs. Germany is a warning. This year it will pay 20 billion euros for wind, solar and biomass power, of which 17 billion euros is subsidy. Big German companies are now investing in the USA because of high power costs at home.

World Wildlife Scotland state: 'Scotland has an opportunity to continue to define itself as a renewables-first, climate-friendly nation.' The cost for such is nowhere mentioned, nor recognition that fuel poverty will increase as renewable development spreads, requiring large subsidies to continue from consumer pockets. Pressure groups now exercise considerable influence over governments, but they lack one important characteristic – they have no responsibility for the consequences of what they argue for.

Scotland's estimated onshore wind resource is 25% of that available to the EU as a whole. Offshore wave resource is 10% of the EU's resource. That is potentially a great advantage, especially in the export of power through interconnection not only with England, but countries in Western Europe. If, however, people are to heat their homes in this northern climate and business is not to be crippled by the cost of electricity, there has to be an objective reassessment about the scale to which Scotland becomes committed to a policy of total reliance on renewables.

Given the advantage, subsidy to wind and wave is unavoidable, but that raises the question of how it is to be continued without its high costs being placed on households and business.

The way forward is a mix of what are regarded as conventional sources: coal, gas and nuclear. Gas is crucial, and it is estimated that Scotland is sitting on huge reserves of shale gas, which can be extracted by the fracking system, which is not a new one. Opponents of fracking can be ignored. They have already engaged in the usual scaremongering, with one anti-fracking web site showing areas being covered in skull & cross bones. That is not science, ignores the wide experience of fracking, and would deprive Scotland of a rich, long term source of very cheap energy, from which cross-subsidisation of renewables could be done without crushing the incomes of people, and damaging business.

A Renewable & On-shore Energy Corporation

There is, unfortunately, no public management and skill base that would allow the successful nationalisation of the renewables industry and its many players. To ensure the build-up of that expertise, the Scottish Government will create a **Renewable & On-shore**

Energy Corporation. It will have the ability to take shares in companies engaged in renewables and shale gas exploitation, and use its position to work with universities to advance research, design, innovation, and manufacturing capacity. The Corporation will work with the SME sector as a new industry is born.

Land Ownership and Land Value Tax

Is it really Scotland's soil?

The pattern of land ownership has history. The poor had no lawyers, and so the land was 'stolen' legally by those who made the laws, and had the lawyers to assist them.

Land is power in rural areas. Power over the local economy, and so, directly or indirectly, over people. The Landowners Association claims that in the great estates, the land is well managed and contributes significantly to the local and national economies. There has been no effective test of these claims. No test as to whether foreign ownership of estates adds or detracts from the potential of the land for public good.

That the present basis of landownership benefits large Scottish landowners and foreign owners is indisputable, considering that a large number use trusts and other opaque instruments for tax purposes, to suit the beneficiaries.

The Duke of Buccleuch does not own Buccleuch Estates, nor does the Queen own Balmoral. In the case of the Duke, the legal ownership is vested in a dormant company Anderson Strathearn Nominees Ltd, with four shareholders, none of whom is a Buccleuch. In the case of the Queen, Balmoral, where she resides in a private capacity, is legally owned by trustees. Other landowners have a more complex set of legal 'veils' making it difficult to identify who really owns the land. Land ownership land use and taxation are intertwined. (source: Andy Wightman 'The Poor Had no Lawyers').

It is not possible for a socialist government to allow the 'something for nothing' substantial financial gains to landowners from hosting wind turbines on their land. The payments they receive, it is necessary to repeat, are from subsidies paid for by consumers, among whom are the elderly, the disabled and low paid workers. Compensation for nationalising the land on which the turbines stand, probably required under human rights legislation, would be costly as the land could no longer be classified as agriculture alone.

The remedy must, therefore, lie in taxation. The tax law will be amended to include a new category: *exceptional unearned income, which will be taxed at 90%.*

Land & Forestry Commission

There will be a New Land & Forestry Act. Its purpose will be to ensure that Scots know who owns Scotland, and can be certain that land and associated resources are used for the economic and social benefit of the nation.

It is a serious question whether with 55% of non-public forests owned by absentees, the prime purpose of these owners is to bring economic benefit to the nation, as distinct from tax avoidance benefit to them. John Clegg and Co., expert advisers on estate and financial planning, inform potential clients that woodland ownership offers a number of tax-efficient benefits. They list them as Business Asset Relief from Inheritance Tax, exemption of increased value in timber from Capital Gains Tax, Capital Gains Roll Over Relief and the fact that 'income generated from the sale of timber from the ownership of commercial woodlands is exempt from both income and corporation tax'.

The new Act will create a Land & Forestry Commission with substantial powers. It will be required to objectively test whether the present landownership and practices, including ownership of forests, are economically and socially beneficial to the nation as a whole, with particular reference to why a great deal of Scottish land, which is on the same latitudes as parts of northern Norway, is much less productive and creates fewer jobs in viable communities.

The commission will bring up to date and make transparent a complete register of land and forest ownership, which will include beneficiaries of any trust or other legal instrument, and it will test whether there is actually valid legal title to land claimed. It is not always certain that a claim is backed by title, as was the case of The Black Cuillin of Skye, where MacLeod of MacLeod made a claim on its whole ownership but could not prove title.

Tenant farmers will have a right to buy to buy their farms at a fair price, thus helping to create a more diverse landownership, and dispersion of power.

The new Act will set out to end Scotland's role in land and forestry as a tax-break haven for wealthy foreigners. After 2016, any foreign person who seeks to buy an estate, agricultural land, or forestry, will be required to have been resident in Scotland for three full years. The 'three year' rule is to ensure that there is a proven commitment to Scotland through the productive development of the land, rather than as now when we see land purchased as a trophy or a tax dodge. Present foreign ownership of estates, agricultural land and forestry, where the beneficiary is a foreign non-resident, will have that ownership converted to 99-year leases. Present holders of land will be free to sell leases, but not ownership of the land which will be vested in the Scottish Government.

Head of State

The people will decide, when creating a written constitution, whether the Windsors will continue to provide Scotland's Head of State. If Scots opt for the Windsors, it is necessary to point out that the present Queen and successors, cannot hold the same position she does today, as the sovereign. Independence makes the people sovereign, and there cannot be another. Therefore the Head of State, if a Windsor, will have a purely ceremonial role, and in all other respects will be a private citizen.

To give effect to this logic policy, the Crown Private Estates Act 1862, which gives special privileges to a sovereign, will be repealed, as will related statutes. As the Head of State will not be a sovereign, arrangements will cease that enable avoidance of inheritance tax (on the basis that bequests from sovereign to sovereign are free from it). A Windsor as head of state will be regarded as a private person in respect of Balmoral and other extensive landholdings (61,000 acres), and subject to all laws applying to all persons.

Time for Land to Pay its Due

Land Value Tax

LVT is a fairer tax than those imposed at present upon houses and businesses. Council tax and business rates will be abolished, and replaced by LVT. Households and businesses will pay only on the rental value of the land their properties stand on. This change will benefit between 75-80% of those paying council tax today.

At present owners of large areas of land, agricultural land, sporting estates, forestry, vacant urban land, pay nothing. That will change with LVT: 4,438,000 hectares of agricultural land, 1,799,783hectares of sporting estates, 1,342,000 hectares of forestry, 2,630 hectares of vacant urban land, will all pay tax for the first time.

LVT levied at 3.16% will see agriculture pay 15.1%, Sporting Estates 0.15%, Forestry 1.12%, vacant urban land 1.37% of the total public revenue from LVT. The effect on household liabilities is redistributive:

	Council Tax £	Land Value Tax £	+/-%
Band A	766	513	-32.9
Band B	894	636	-28.8
Band C	1,021	820	-20
Band G	1,915	3,261	+69.7

(source: Wightman: Paper for Scottish Green Party).

Public expenditure on infrastructure raises the value of adjacent land with no return to the community. As Churchill in his Liberal days said, the landowner sits, does nothing, but reaps a dividend. It can be a considerable dividend.

In London the £3.5 billion public investment improving transport infastructure caused a £13.5 billion increase in land values along its route. In Scotland, the status of the Cairngorms National Park raised land values there. The Borders railway, offering quicker access to Edinburgh and the onward rail network, will do the same.

Jobs, Contracts and Wages

The measures outlined here aim to create jobs and move Scotland to full employment. But the creation of jobs per se, is not enough. Jobs with high wages are needed.

Working tax credits and any replacement will be phased out over five years. These are spun as subsidies to people in work whose wages are low. They are, in fact, a direct subsidy to employers who have no incentive to improve wage levels. Low wages, subsidies from taxpayers, is a formula for a low wage economy. That this truth should pass by the present Labour leadership is an indication of how Blairite New Labour has destroyed the intellectual foundation of that party. Milliband is offering a tax cut to employers if they will pay workers the living wage. That pathetic suggestion is an example of what happens when a left-wing party loses its ideological compass.

The minimum wage will be replaced by a 'living wage' in the public sector immediately a socialist government is installed, and upgraded to a 'living wage' in the private sector as working tax credits are phased out.

That 'living wage' will be raised in line with inflation, plus 1% in the first two years, and by 2% from years three to five in the phasing out of working tax credits.

It cannot be over emphasised that if Scotland is to flourish in the global community, it cannot be as a low-wage, low-productivity, low-skilled, part-time labour force nation. The public policy outlined above is designed to drive up the international quality of our business base, which will require appropriate levels of sustained investment, all of which are a precursor to higher wages paid to people.

It can be anticipated that this policy will produce assertions that the rise in employer costs will mean fewer jobs, as employers struggle to pay. It is interesting to note that the same argument about the negative effect on business of improved worker conditions was prayed in aid when, in the nineteenth century, it was decided to cut the hours of ten-year-olds in factories down to 10 hours per day. Lo and behold, the industrial revolution and employer profit were not affected.

Contracts Will Favour the Worker

Contracts of employment are often misunderstood as being in some special category. They are like any other commercial contract, in that an agreement is signed to exchange money, not for goods, but for labour. Where they are different is that labour is in the weak position of having to sign whether the person so doing is happy with the contract, because of the need for a job. This is especially the case in times of high unemployment. The contract was of no use to the Grangemouth workers. It was torn up by the management.

Zero-hours contracts illustrate this. People desperate for work have very little choice. They are treated not as human beings, but as a commodity, as a shopper would treat a can of beans on a supermarket shelf, to be picked up or left on a 'shelf' as an employer pleases. This is exploitation of a human being, and it will be a criminal offence to offer a contract of less than 16 hours per week.

All contracts of employment will have a clause, assuring the worker that he or she can join a trade union of their choice. It will be a criminal offence, not a civil offence, if an employer places any pressure on workers to ignore their rights as set out in the contract. In addition to any criminal penalties, compensation will be paid, through the Industrial Tribunal system for any worker sacked for seeking trade union membership, engaging in recruiting new members, or engaging in trade union activities.

A More Just and Equal Society

If there is no control over incomes in a society where the workers are weak, then gross inequality develops. This has been the case for Scotland as part of the UK. As we have seen in banks, big business, the BBC, and local government, the top management, which can reward itself, does so without any display of conscience

The poorest tenth in Scotland own 2% of total income. The second poorest tenth own 4%. The richest tenth own 29%. The second richest tenth own 15%. The richest tenth's income is equal to all those on the bottom five tenths. The gap between the rich and the rest has been growing. Steps will be taken to adjust to a more equal society through taxation and other policies.

In the public sector, there will be a statutory rule that the highest paid person in the organisation will not be paid thirteen times more than the wages of the lowest paid worker. That will be phased in over 5 years. Bonus payments in the public sector will cease. There is no justification for senior officials getting a bonus for doing the jobs they are paid for. These policies should have a salutary effect upon restoring the concept of public service, something that many at the top seem to have forgotten.

The 'living wage' will become mandatory in the private sector five years after independence, thus giving employers time to adjust their business plans.

Payday Loans

Ideally pay-day loan companies should be banned. However, within Europe and beyond, finance knows no boundaries. Nothing, for example, could stop a person in Scotland contracting a pay-day loan from a company in England. But a socialist government would not be powerless. These companies can be curbed, by capping the level of interest. A cap equal to three times the average interest charged on a credit card would seem reasonable, given the higher degree of risk involved. This is, of course, advocacy of interfering with the free market. As Wayne A.M.Visser and Alastair McIntosh pointed out in a paper on usury, Adam Smith, yes he himself, was 'in favour of the imposition of an interest-rate ceiling.'

A Policy for Small Business & international Trade

'Micro, small and medium-sized enterprises are the engine of the European economy ... an essential source of jobs, create entrepreneurial spirit and innovation.'
European Commission

SMEs are defined as 10-250 employees. Lip service, echoing the European Commission, is often paid to them. Modifications to general business policies in their favour come forward from time to time, but there has not been a policy that seeks to drive this business community forward and up the value chain in a dynamic way. Access to capital and credit can be a considerable barrier to the creation or expansion of an SME.

Often, a small company exists when someone has taken a risk with their own money and built the company with hard work and very low personal returns in the early stages. We need more people to take this risk.

SMEs do not threaten the national or local economy. They are part of it, and their contribution must not only be valued, but encouraged to continue with government policy tailored to spread the SME net wider, and ensure that the risk taken is not punished when success comes.

Innovation is one of the key factors in SMEs developing and becoming successful. That often requires reinvestment of profits, especially over the early years of a new project. Encouragement of innovation and job creation lies at the heart of this programme's SME policy. For the SME sector throughout Scotland, there will be no capital gains tax. Employer national insurance will be reduced by 50%. Access to finance will be through an SME publicly owned bank, and Land Value Tax will remove the penalties inherent in the present business tax system.

Big companies in both the domestic and international markets can look after themselves. That is not always the case for the smaller companies in respect of efforts to trade abroad, and access capital and credit at home.

This programme has set out how the state will create jobs. That will not be enough in a drive towards full employment. It is to the 339,110 SMEs (2012 fig.), employing 1.09 million people, that we must look for jobs at levels the economy and our people require.

The SMEs account for 54.5% of private sector employment and 37.7% of private sector turnover. Their development is essential in the creation of more jobs. So, helping them within the framework of employment protection as set out previously is a matter of national priority.

Some in the SME sector will wonder at these comments, given this is a socialist programme, where great emphasis is laid on protecting and empowering workers. But as was set out very early in the text, socialism cannot be a dogma, or be blind to the realities that capital comes in many forms, and that the SME sector is in a different class of capital from the multi-nationals – that it forms part of the community and serves the community as well as the persons who invested in it.

An SME Bank

As events since 2007 have proved, what hampers the development of the SME sector, is its low priority in that normal source of capital and credit finance – the Banks. If a society is serious about the importance of the SMES, then it will take action to meet their needs.

The Scottish Socialist Government will create an SME Bank. It will act on the principle that credit unions use: people contribute to its capital formation as a condition for drawing credit.

The SME Bank will be funded initially by the Government, which will inject capital and appoint one-third of the Board, and by a special levy at a percentage of turnover from each SME for two years running, and a lower percentage in subsequent years. The Federation of Small Business will nominate from its membership to the Board, and they will fill one-third. The final third of the Board will be drawn from local government and public enterprises.

The Bank's function will be to manage credit to the SME sector. The remuneration of top management will be on the 13-1 ratio as for all other public sector organisations.

An SME Ministry

This will be at cabinet rank. This Ministry will ensure that all government policy assists, and does no harm, to the development of the public goal of a successful and prosperous SME sector.

It will have specific responsibility to ensure that the necessary training, back-up, research, logistical and financial assistance is available to SMEs through a major state-funded programme that takes them into foreign markets. It is difficult for SMEs seeking for the first time to step into a foreign country to export products or services. There has to be market research, visits where the culture and business practices differ from ours, and repeat visits where contacts need to be built over time, which is expensive in cash and time.

At home the SME sector will get priority. R&D is an SME weakness. The new Ministry will have a new role to play in assisting the SME sector, through liaison with Universities, to address this problem.

A successful policy of support for the 339,000 SMEs would see, with even half of them employing two more persons, a substantial creation of jobs

Train Operating Companies

Kevin Lindsay of ASLEF has pointed the way in the **Red Paper on Scotland 2014.** Simply wait until the TOC franchise runs out, and take it into public ownership at no cost. That will be the policy.

During the continuing franchise, given the importance of rail as part of the economic infrastructure, the Government will appoint public interest directors to the Board of the train operating company.

The Post Office

This has to be treated differently. Confiscation of private companies is held to be offensive, an outrage against private right. Confiscation of public property, however, seems to invite no condemnation. The Royal Mail is a classic example of the latter. It was owned by the people, yet 70% was confiscated. Royal Mail not only delivers mail, but owns a large number of valuable properties that, if action is not taken, will be sold well above the notional value in the privatisation prospectus.

Taking back what was ours is the policy. The Scottish Post Office will be renationalised. Shares will be swapped for non-interest bearing bonds, maturing for payment in five years

Taxation

There is a combination of principles and necessity in taxation. Income tax is progressive and redistributive, but that base alone cannot meet government expenditure. Indirect taxes, regressive though they may be, are part of a required tax base.

Income tax: the higher rate will rise to 55% on incomes over £150,000. No one earning less than £12,000 will pay income tax.

Vat: 20% rate will be lowered to 18%, but raised to 30% on luxury goods.

Corporation tax: there will be no reduction in the rate of 20% (2015) for large companies, but lowered to 15% for SMEs.

Multinationals have tied governments in knots, using diverse structures and tax havens. Government agreement to an international rule will fail. Vested interests and powerful lobbies will see to that.

EU law, which applies throughout the European Economic Area, allows multinationals to choose a low tax base location in which to declare profits. This enables them to pay a very low tax on profits in a country in which the profits were not earned. The TUC has pointed out that every 47p of any £1 spent on bananas in a UK supermarket, ends up in a tax haven. The EU/EEA situation rules out taxing them on the basis of their sales in Scotland.

That sovereign governments should be in this position where the Amazons and Starbucks can pay next to nothing while claiming, correctly, that they are not breaking any laws, makes a mockery of the democratic mandate. The multinationals who engage in tax dodging are breaking the normal rules of society that are, in the words of the TUC, 'fundamental to civilised life – no tax income, no government, no society.'

But, bearing in mind the Nye Bevan dictum to think and act audaciously, sovereign power can be used to get what society deserves. If taxation is impossible, **licensing is not.** Any multi-national operating in Scotland will be required to have a licence to trade. It is obvious the licence cannot be based on a company's sales or notional profits. That would be a poorly disguised tax, and fall foul of EU/EEA law. No, the licence will be based on a variety of objective factors that arise from the public benefits the company gets, which are disproportionate to what it pays in land value tax. What will determine the licence fee is the location and size of properties, their function, number of employees, employee use of public transport, employee use of private transport, employee use of health services, the companies' heavy vehicle use of roads, water, electricity, gas, and protection from the law enforcement agencies.

The Welfare State

The welfare state has been under severe attack. It is an irony that politicians who support the market-based system that destroyed the manufacturing base, creating great pools of human misery, should blame the victims for their condition. It is perhaps not surprising that it was from a New Labour mouth that the scornful 'something for nothing' gibe was directed at those who are protected by the welfare state.

It isn't a financial whip on the backs of the poor, single mothers, the disabled, that will successfully reduce the welfare bill. It is good paying jobs and a superb educational foundation for each child that will accomplish that. Work that pays good wages is what will make it worthwhile to get into work.

There will be no dismantling of the welfare state or universal benefits in a socialist Scotland. The intellectual underpinning for that policy is to be found in the publications by the Jimmy Reid Foundation.

Social Security Benefits. There will never be a bedroom tax. The disabled and sick will be treated with respect, and cuts imposed on them will be restored. There will be no more humiliation of disabled people in front of tribunals whose purpose is to cut expenditure, not care for those who need our understanding, compassion and help.

The complexities of the Tory Government's Job Seekers Allowances, which claims to assist people into work where, however, no work exists, will be scrapped.

It will be replaced by unemployment benefit. For those who have no national insurance contributions it will be doubled. For those who have been in work for two years, and have made insurance contributions, the rate will be 75% of their last annual wage for two years, with the right to retraining paid for by the state, reducing to 60% of their annual wage in the next two years, and 50% of the annual wage in all subsequent years. They will be expected to pay national insurance contributions from the unemployment benefit. This policy, for individuals, will ensure that there is no dramatic drop in living standards when a job is lost, and in the national interest no dramatic drop in the cash for spending in local economies.

State Pension. There is one outstanding fact in the pensions debate that is ignored: the only organisation that can guarantee a pension in retirement is the state, which has the necessary powers to do so.

Some 17% of Scottish single male pensioners, and 18% of single female pensioners are living in poverty. A number entitled to pension credit do not claim. For some the means test is obnoxious. There is no other way to end pensioner poverty except by paying a pension that takes them out of it. The basic pension today is £110.15 per week, £5,727 a year. The proposed £144 per week will, in effect, taking inflation into account, be £155 in 2016. That will not take pensioners out of poverty, nor will a pension of £160 per week. A socialist government will *raise the basic state pension to the level that will take all pensioners out of poverty with a state pension of £178 per week.*

As the state pension is a taxable income, part of that increase will be taken back into the Scottish Finance Ministry, but the level ensures that no pensioner will live in poverty. This increase will be funded by lifting the ceiling on national insurance contributions, increased income tax on the rich, VAT at 30% on luxury goods, and general taxation.

The Unionists will cry 'look at the demographics'. Leaving aside the little matter that they seem unconcerned or unable to deal with the growing gap between the rich and poor, and the level of poverty among pensioners, the error they fall into is to see the economy as a static thing – the same 'cake' simply divided differently, with an increase in one state payment meaning a consequent cut in another area of expenditure. That is the case in devolution, where there is a bloc grant to be distributed. It is not the case with independence, where the opportunity arises to grow the economy and make that 'cake' (GDP and state revenues) much bigger, and therefore better able to meet essential social spend such as state pensions.

There have been so many declared wars on poverty it is amazing that there is any left … but there is – lots of it – and the reason is that what can be done to eradicate it has not been done.

Bus pass. The free bus pass will no longer apply to those aged between 60 and 64. This will not save a great deal, £10 million a year, but you can do a lot with that elsewhere. As explained in relation to funding for Sistema.

Winter fuel allowance. For those who qualify and live alone, an increase from £200 to £300. For the over-eighties increased from £300 to £400. This allowance, like the state pension, will be taxable. That deals with the issue of people getting it whose income level shows they do not need it, while guaranteeing that those who do need it, get it.

Women and legal aid. The provision of free nursery education will be a benefit to mothers working or seeking work, as will the upgrading of the minimum and living wages, and laws on hours offered in a contract. Women facing domestic violence need adequate legal advice. The legal aid fund will be divided between a general fund, and a domestic violence fund. The latter will be a generous fund with rules that will guarantee no woman subjected to domestic violence goes without legal advice.

The NHS

So far, with Holyrood control of the NHS it is not subject to the privatisation now taking place in England where market forces have been unleashed, and advisors to companies are boasting of £6 billion available for private bidding. However, if we remain with devolution, even one where some tax-raising powers are operative, there will still be a bloc grant required from the Westminster government. As the crunch of cuts descends after the 2015 election, the Scottish Government's finances will be cut in real terms. There will then be pressure to go down the English road. *The maintenance of the NHS as a public service is paramount.*

There are three key facts about the NHS: (1) its singular purpose is to heal the sick and injured; no other health provider can say the same; (2) the public sector ethos that its staff provides is a value beyond calculation; (3) notwithstanding the public sector ethos, the NHS is a monopoly provider, and, therefore, has a tendency to spawn self-serving bureaucracies. While a firm commitment can be given to support the NHS as a government priority, no public monopoly can sensibly be ring-fenced. Consistent and stringent audit examinations will be carried out.

A particular welcome is given to the decision of the SNP Government to have seven-day working in hospitals

PFI. The NHS was taken to the cleaners when the PFI contracts were negotiated, due largely to the inexperience of those on the public side. These PFI contracts are a serious drain on the NHS (and education) budget. Between 2013-14 and 2041, the Scottish public sector will pay out to PFI/PPP providers £24.2467 billion.

The aim will be to renegotiate each one, reducing payments substantially by at least 30%. If the PFI providers refuse to renegotiate, they will *be subject to a yearly excess-profits tax*. The NHS had poor lawyers last time in terms of experience, but not this time. The people's power in backing a socialist government will see that power used legally in the public interest.

Conclusion

Not only has Scotland's people been kept in a prison of lies about the oil wealth, they have had their self-belief consistently attacked through the creation of the idea that they are inadequate. It was no accident that the No side described their campaign as 'Project Fear'. On every count, on every policy, the No campaign would have Scots believe they are tragically unique: that they alone in this world are incapable of running their own country, and must hand over themselves as permanent supplicants to control by another nation.

No campaigners frequently claim that Scotland is part of the most successful union the world has seen. If measured by its imperial reach in the past, that is true. But the UK has not been a success for more than half a century, as it retreated from empire. Economic crisis after economic crisis has been the sorry tale from 1945 onwards. The so-called Thatcher revolution led to the crisis of deindustrialisation, the unleashing of greed in the financial sector, and ultimately to the shambles that was the Major-Blair-Brown years. A national debt heading for £1.5 trillion, and the dishonest resort to growth through more debt, puts the lie to that foolish claim.

Independence is an opportunity to rid ourselves of the repeated failures that have been our lot as part of a British state in its final phases of decline. The price of remaining with that state for individual Scots is too high. Whether it be a single parent, a pensioner, a disabled person, a student with qualifications, a worker, the UK is a 'no hope' land.

This socialist programme is for people who have had enough of failure. People who are ambitious, who know they are intelligent, who are confident about this nation's collective ability, and who are determined to sweep aside the crippling myth of inadequacy, and enter a new age where a fairer, decent society can be built because it values co-operation, communities and rejects greed.

In September, using the sovereign power that will lie in their hands as they pick up that ballot paper, the people should remember the words of that old miner in Netherthird, and resolve that never again will our policies for the working people be destroyed by the London connection. We have it in us to create a harmonious, prosperous, outward-looking nation dedicated to the principles of fairness and social justice. All we need is a Yes vote.

Postscript

Europe

In which European context is this programme cast? It is difficult to understand why the SNP Government opted for a one-club policy – continued membership of the EU. I was the author of the Independence in Europe policy. But that was in the 1980s, with the EU small in number of member states, and veto powers widely available. The EU is now gigantic, veto powers are few, and the power of the Commission in the Eurozone has, over member states' budgets, all but eliminated their sovereignty.

The dispute over Scotland and the EU, and the terms the latter will set for our continued membership, will rage for some time, and the mystery is why the SNP Government has not opted for the alternative, which is EFTA. Membership of EFTA gives what Scotland needs, access through the European Economic Area (a joint agreement between EFTA and EU) to the whole European market, and the ability to exercise a greater range of sovereign powers than is available as a member of the EU. Scotland is an easy fit with EFTA – small in numbers, oil producer, and fisheries resource.

Even if the SNP Cabinet would choose the EU over EFTA, it seems sensible that the EFTA alternative would provide a good bargaining position. A wise leadership, aware that 5 million people cannot dictate terms of membership to twenty-eight others representing 500 million, would have made diplomatic contacts with EFTA countries some years ago, and certainly since 2011. That did not happen. The SNP position will, therefore, be subject to whatever attitude is struck by the powers in Brussels, giving them the upper hand in negotiations.

This programme does not take the SNP line, nor should the people of Scotland. Membership of EFTA will not free Scotland from much of the regulation required for all in the EEA, but EFTA members exercise sovereignty over their own budgets, fisheries, foreign policy, and trade policy with the rest of the world, to mention but a few state activities.

Common sense on defence

Foreign and defence policy are intertwined. The relevance of both in this document is in relation to some of the policies it spells out. Scotland will not seek to project hard military power. Its foreign policy will emphasise humanitarian engagement with the rest of the world, and building trade relations.

Fact: Scotland does not have a single state enemy. No state threatens us with invasion. The one threat, shared by many other states, is that from non-state actors, terrorists, who direct their attacks at civil society and national economic assets. It follows that we do not need a cut-down UK defence model.

The need in Scotland is a fleet of specialised ships, built in Scottish yards, to guard our coastlines against drug smuggling and entry from the sea by terrorists, and protect the North Sea rigs. In addition we require a small army from which to draw special forces able to deal with attacks on the oil installations.

The point of independence is that it means change, big change, and one of the big changes is that we start to refocus our relationship with others, where our influence will come from soft power – aiding people instead of killing them

No Single Police Force

A single police force should be anathema to any democrat. No claims about savings should be allowed to create one, even if it were true, which will probably not be the case.

The police is not a service, it is a force, the coercive force of the state. To diminish the potential for that force to be used for illegitimate purposes, it has to be divided not centralised. The single police force will be replaced by four police authorities.

Appendix

This is the list of the main policy proposals in the programme:-
- A Scottish currency. No currency union.
- A Monetary Authority – no independent central bank
- A different economic model based on resource management
- Living wage upgrading. Phasing out of minimum wage
- Greater protection for workers
- Innovative use of bonds, including sukuks
- Taxation and the need for redistribution
- Free nursery school place for every child from one to five years in deprived areas
- Free place for every child in other areas from thee to five years
- Teachers: status raised and paid better
- Thirty-two local education authorities replaced by five Joint Boards
- Primary & Secondaries in multiple deprivation areas to get double per capita
- Students at S3 able to transfer to Higher Technical Institutes
- State schools to be given charitable status
- FE Colleges' status enhanced to that of Higher Technical Institutes
- Awarding Technical Baccalaureates
- University funding to make Scotland the outstanding scientific centre of Europe

- Funding for tertiary education by progressive steps increasing to 2.8% of GDP
- A pre-university College to prevent the high drop out rate continuing
- Jobs: creation of Scottish Environmental Engineering Corps
- Jobs: creation of a Housing Development Authority to build 25,000 homes a year
- Jobs: creation of an SME Ministry and SME bank
- Creation of Scottish Hospital Ship & international Rescue Service, using
- second redundant aircraft carrier to be named The Robert Burns
- Creation of young international volunteer group Scottish Overseas Service
- A Scottish National Oil Corporation with authority to buy oil companies
- Scottish North Sea Directorate to deal with greater share of decommissioning
- Inserting public interest into public utilities
- Reduction in fuel duties to boost economy
- Radical land reform – including change in status of the Queen
- Women: legal aid to have domestic violence fund separate from general fund
- Increase to winter fuel allowance
- Increase of state pension
- No bus pass for 60-64 age group

Acknowledgements

I would like to thank Professor Joe Farrell, who was chairman of the SLP, without whose encouragement and consistent support I would not have undertaken this work.

I also want to thank my wife Margo MacDonald MSP and her Office Manager Peter Warren, a personal friend. They have been more than helpful in ensuring that my thoughts did not become tangled, and that my research was accurate.